A New Ladies' Man

A
**Complete
Guide
to Getting,
Pleasing, and
Keeping the Girl**

Colin Mortensen

A Perigee/**Razorbill Book**

THE BERKLEY PUBLISHING GROUP
Published by the Penguin Group
Penguin Group (USA) Inc.
375 Hudson Street, New York, New York 10014, USA
Penguin Group (Canada), 90 Eglinton Avenue East, Suite 700, Toronto, Ontario M4P 2Y3, Canada
(a division of Pearson Penguin Canada Inc.)
Penguin Books Ltd., 80 Strand, London WC2R 0RL, England
Penguin Group Ireland, 25 St. Stephen's Green, Dublin 2, Ireland (a division of Penguin Books Ltd.)
Penguin Group (Australia), 250 Camberwell Road, Camberwell, Victoria 3124, Australia
(a division of Pearson Australia Group Pty. Ltd.)
Penguin Books India Pvt. Ltd., 11 Community Centre, Panchsheel Park, New Delhi—110 017, India
Penguin Group (NZ), cnr. Airborne and Rosedale Roads, Albany, Auckland 1310, New Zealand
(a division of Pearson New Zealand Ltd.)
Penguin Books (South Africa) (Pty.) Ltd., 24 Sturdee Avenue, Rosebank, Johannesburg 2196,
South Africa
Penguin Books Ltd., Registered Offices: 80 Strand, London WC2R 0RL, England

ISBN: 0-399-530878

PRINTING HISTORY
Perigee trade paperback edition / November 2005

PERIGEE is a registered trademark of Penguin Group (USA) Inc.
The "P" design is a trademark belonging to Penguin Group (USA) Inc.

This book has been cataloged by the Library of Congress.

PRINTED IN THE UNITED STATES OF AMERICA

10   9   8   7   6   5   4   3   2   1

Kangaroos have two vaginas.

Scratch and sniff.

*To my grandparents, Fernando and Carolina Sánchez,
in celebration of their fifty-seven-year love affair.*

Contents

A New Ladies' Man

Introduction

Sex.

Sex?

Sex!

Now I've got your attention. I set out to write a sex book for guys when I was twenty years old—a little black book that young dudes would secretly pass around to each other at school when the teacher wasn't looking. The book you have in your hands, *A New Ladies' Man*, became something much bigger. It morphed into a guide to becoming a modern man, one who has no problem getting attention from the ladies because he understands one important rule: *If you learn how to give women what they want, then more women will want you.*

I was clueless about women and sex while growing up and, like most guys, I had very few people in my life who I was willing to turn to for truthful and accurate information. My friends were just as clueless as I was. My parents (as nice, open, and informed as they were) were not the people I wanted to talk to about girls and sex. (I couldn't really picture going up to my mother at the age of fifteen and saying, "Mom, can you teach me how to go down on a girl with the use of personal anecdotes?") My older brother didn't seem too concerned with my overall development, either; he was too busy pinning me down and letting his spit dribble onto my face.

I spent too many years wondering how I was going to get the girl of my dreams, whether my zits were going to clear up, and when I was going to stop masturbating and start hooking up with actual living, breathing girls (outside of my imagination). I spent too much time absorbing the images from our culture, which encourage men to be selfish, unfeeling, and out of touch, before I realized there was another way—*a better way*.

I didn't want other guys to have to go through the same clouded, dark, and ignorant nonsense that I did, so I started writing.

If you are a guy reading this book, I want you to think of yourself as a 7' × 7' solid piece of marble. Somewhere within that mass of rock lies a Ladies' Man. Within these pages, I will hand you some of the tools you need to chisel yourself into the statuesque image of a modern man.

Sick of getting tongue-tied and sounding like a human boner when you try to ask a girl out? Carve out a tongue that will say all the right things. Curious about sex? Wondering about how to develop style and become part of the social scene? Use the chisel to contour your image and personality.

A New Ladies' Man gives you practical day-to-day advice. Like how to hide your public hard-ons. How to tell if the size and shape of your dick and balls are normal. How to lessen your fears about dating and having a girlfriend. How to determine whether it's normal to masturbate thirty times a day.

Finally, this book will give you solid tips on how to kiss a girl, touch a girl, lick a girl, have sex with a girl, and bring a girl to orgasm.

Each piece of information that you take in and apply to your life chips away at that solid piece of rock, until all that remains is the striking presence of you: a unique and confident Ladies' Man.

While doing the market research for *A New Ladies'*

Hey ladies,

I would like to point out that *A New Ladies' Man* is also intended to be appreciated by *you.*

This book is a tribute to women. But beyond that, this book provides a look inside the minds of the young men you are dating, having sex with, and planning to have sex with.

The crap running through our heads is not always pretty, but with this book, you can gain the insight that will help you show even the most clueless dude the path to becoming a Ladies' Man.

Most importantly, if you're not dating anyone right now, I hope that this book illustrates the kind of guy you should be looking for—the kind of guy you deserve—which is, above all, a person who is *giving*—sexually, emotionally, and spiritually. (For example, *me.* Call me, ladies. You know the number.)

Man I noticed a trend. Most of the books out there for guys like us are written by older women. I wanted you guys to have something to read that was written by a dude who had actually been down the path. *Me*. What I have to say in this book might not be brilliant and it might not be true for everyone, but it sure as hell would have helped me when I was confused and trying to figure things out for myself.

So now it's time to turn you into a sex god; but before we do that, I would like to point out that I am not a medical doctor. A doctor of love? Perhaps. Do I own scrubs? Yes. Have I been known to use a stethoscope on a lady or two in my day? (Hey, stay out of my business.) The point is that I've never gone to medical school, and I didn't even know how to spell *stethoscope,* let alone properly handle one, until yesterday (sorry, ladies). In short, this book is not intended to be medical advice, nor is it intended to be a substitute for consulting with your physician or other health care providers. Any serious issues in relation to your physical, mental, and emotional health should be supervised by appropriate professionals. Not me.

So read on, and let's get it started.

PART 1

Get 'Em Interested

First on the agenda, our mission statement: The goal of this book is to teach you how to meet, attract, and develop relationships (kick-ass relationships) with girls.

But before you get to approach a girl, or attempt to hook up with her, you've got to get your act together and learn to understand your own body. If you don't understand yourself, then you're likely to fall flat on your face with girls. (Or at least that's what I've heard. I wouldn't know from personal experience or anything.)

This chapter will teach you some vital information about yourself and your body, from how it can be your best friend to how it can sell you out faster than an undercover cop posing as a two-dollar hooker.

In the Developing Style section—or, as I like to call it, *A Refined Straight Eye for the Young Guy*—I will give you advice about clothes and shoes (what to wear and where to find these items), cooking for a girl (a great way to get her over to your house), musical choices (what to play around girls, whether you're hooking up or hanging out), and why *not* to wear tighty-whities. I also discuss guys who go commando (without underwear)—and in doing so let their dicks flop around all day in close proximity to their hazardous zippers.

Then we move on to Your Penis and You, where you will learn what the size of your dick has to do with the likelihood of getting some action. You will also discover the truth about shrinkage, semis, boners, and why masturbation kicks ass. Oh yeah, and I've provided you with a place to plaster your balls to my book at the end of this section.

The final section of part one is Making the First Move. This is where we get to the good stuff. Here you will learn how to create an "in" with a girl—a situation that will allow you to get to know her, get her phone number, and eventually ask her out. We will also discuss how your level of confidence affects the way that girls view you and respond to you, what dancing does for the ladies, how to party your balls off, and what to do when you get a boner on the dance floor. Lastly, I tackle the mysterious "mangina."

1

Developing Style

*"It's always been one of my greatest goals
in life to look good."*
—MY MOTHER, SUSAN SÁNCHEZ

Does having style make you a man?

No.

Does having style make you kind?

No.

Does having style make you compassionate?

No.

However, having style *does* increase the possibility
that women all around the world will be tattooing your
name on their asses! (Well, not really, but you get the
point.) Developing style to attract a girl isn't a very

"deep" change to make in your life. In fact, it's down-right shallow. Nonetheless, it's effective and a first step toward getting women to notice you.

I would like to point out that, as a young dude, I was clueless when it came to being stylish. How clueless? Let's just say that I parted my hair down the middle for the first nineteen years of my life—and I secured the middle part by plastering it to my head with the strongest holding gel on the face of the planet. Next to me, Harry Potter would've looked like the male model of the year.

Which is to say, I started off in a much worse position than most of you, stylewise. So have no fear. Even if you have no clue about what to wear, there is hope for you all.

So how do you develop style?

I've got one word for you: *Strateegery*.

Clothes

Clothes are a big part of your overall style because they give girls an impression of what you're like before you get to open your mouth. Their impression *before* the impression. Let me set the scene for you: A girl sees you across the room. You see her across the room. She checks out your mock-worn-in Abercrombie & Fitch T-shirt and your store-bought ripped jeans, and thinks, "Boring."

You could be the greatest person on the planet—you could be this girl's *soul mate*—but there isn't a shot in hell that she's going to give you a second glance. Why? Because you look exactly like the next guy.

Is it fair? Not really. But let's be honest, we don't see a girl standing across the way and say, "Wow, she's got a great personality." We notice other things first. Yes, of course, *those* things, but we also notice a girl's style and demeanor.

Some people think having style is about wearing what everyone else is wearing. You know, just buy the uniform shirt and khakis from the Gap and blend in, right? Wrong. Each Ladies' Man is unique. Therefore, each Ladies' Man should work toward developing a style that fits his body, his personality, and his lifestyle.

You have to ask yourself which clothes fit *you* well. That's when you will truly have style. *Your* style. Which is good, because women dig it when you're original.

The confidence you have in yourself and your clothes is what sells your style. Don't let anybody tell you that you don't look good if you think you do. It's your style. Not theirs.

Be your own man.

What To Wear

Guys have the luxury of being able to look great in simple clothing.

Women love classic style, like a nice pair of jeans and a fitted T-shirt, so let's start there: Pick a pair of jeans with a medium or dark blue wash. You want your jeans to fit your waist so that you have a little room to put your thumb in between the jean button and your belly button. You should be able to wear your jeans without a belt. This doesn't mean that you can't (or shouldn't) wear a belt, but the ability to wear them without the support of accessories should give you a clear indication of how your jeans should fit your waist. Your jeans should rest on the outside of the tongue on your shoes (not tucked inside of the tongue à la Zack Morris from the eighties sitcom *Saved by the Bell*), and they should break against the top of your shoe (meaning, they should kind of bend inward, toward your leg) only once. If your jeans are creating four or five folds instead of breaking once, they are too long.

Fifty-fifty (50 percent cotton and 50 percent polyester) is the classic blend for T-shirts. They are more comfortable, they look better, and they age better than 100 percent cotton shirts. You can find out what fabric a T-shirt is made of by checking the tag on the back of the neck.

In the classic style, T-shirts shouldn't be too big. Instead, they should fit your body without an excess of fabric. However, T-shirts also shouldn't be too tight. If someone can accurately trace your nipples, areola, and belly button on the outside of your T-shirt, then you need to go one size up. What you're aiming for is the middle of the road, fitwise. Go for a solid color T-shirt, or a baseball-style shirt (the kind where the sleeves are a

"Cash rule' everythang around me."
—Mos Def

Contrary to popular belief, your jeans do *not* have to be designer. I know people who spend hundreds of dollars on their jeans. This is like throwing your money into a fire pit. Girls don't like you because of the name brand on your ass. If this were true, then even *my* friends could get some action—but they strike out wearing Diesels all the time. So that you know, I buy my jeans at American Eagle. They cost twenty-five dollars, and they fit me perfectly.

different color than the rest of the body.) Throw on a pair of cool sneakers (the kind you wear for hanging out—not for playing ball), and you have achieved a classic style.

Now that we've got that covered, let's talk about how to change up that style to make it your own. Try out one or more of the styles below and see what works for you.

YOUR SCENE / STYLE IDEAS

Hip-hop/urban Go for styles that are a little baggier. Rock some shirts and jerseys with athletic motifs. Or channel Diddy and try a smoother look with collared shirts.

Environmentally conscious Choose clothing made with hemp, or recycled materials, in earthy tones, with a relaxed fit. Also, check out the ethnic styles of Mexico and South America.

Artistic Customize your clothes with your own designs or browse the vintage stores for one-of-a-kind items (Western dress shirts, seventies dress shirts and polyester dress pants, old T-shirts with funny or interesting logos, etc.). Women notice original style.

Punk Pick up some different-colored Dickies (pants), skate shoes, a fitted hat, and throw on a long-sleeved shirt with a short-sleeved T-shirt over it: This is a classic southern California style.

I like to express myself through clothing by wearing T-shirts with a funny or provocative message. (This has the added benefit of being an instant conversation-starter when you're around the ladies.) For example, when I wear my EVERY MOTHER IS A WORKING MOTHER T-shirt or my WHEN I GROW UP I WANNA BE A HOOTERS GIRL T-shirt, then I know I'm going to receive some attention from women. Giving a girl a reason to talk to you is a wise move.

Another way that I ensure that my clothes are original is by buying most of them at thrift stores. Not only are the styles more interesting, they're also cheaper than retail clothing.

Today, at a thrift store, I bought a corduroy suit (matching pants and jacket) with chocolate suede elbow patches, a white tuxedo shirt with pink stripes and French cuffs, and a three-piece Italian suit (with an orange silk vest). I paid twelve dollars for the corduroy suit, four dollars for the tuxedo shirt, and five dollars for the Italian suit. Total expense: twenty-one dollars.

I also find clothing while traveling. I have clothes from county fairs in the middle of the United States, and clothes from other countries.

Now, I'm not saying that you have to be like me and wear a full seventies corduroy suit to your friend's party (although if you did, I would be impressed) or that you have to go to the Yucatán Peninsula to buy your shirts (I wasn't able to do that until I became a thousandaire): Just buy clothing that is interesting (instead of the same Abercrombie & Fitch T-shirt that half the guys in America are wearing). Women notice you when you are confident and original. So don't be a sheep. There are enough sheep in the world. Be a shepherd. Let them follow you.

In addition to your casual look you will also want to own a handful of funky, collared, long-sleeved dress shirts to wear out for dressier occasions (like a date or a school dance). In those instances, you're also going to need something else. Something girls can't help but notice . . .

Shoes

Women love shoes.

Now I know you're thinking, "All right, I'll get one pair of nice shoes and I'll just wear them every time I go out."

Survey says . . .

NO!

One of my best friends recently became a lawyer. He told me that the first thing the partners of his law firm told him was to buy several extremely expensive pairs of shoes. Needless to say, he was baffled. What do shoes have to do with law? The senior partner explained to him that female jurors notice shoes. If you have an extraordinarily nice pair, it gives them a good impression of you as a person, which, in turn, helps your case.

Do your shoes make you a better man or a better lawyer?

No.

Do girls look for them?

Yes.

So don't fight it.

You should have, at minimum, four core pairs of shoes. One: a nice pair of cross-trainers (some stores call these "lifestyle sneakers") to wear with your jeans when you are going casual. Two: a pair of sneakers for working out, playing basketball, etc. Three: a black pair of dress shoes that will go with your jeans or with any pair of dress pants for school dances, clubs, or special occasions. Four: a pair of chocolate-brown dress shoes that can go with your jeans and all the other dressy/funky outfits that are not appropriate to wear with black dress shoes.

Your dress shoes don't have to be shiny, stiff, and uncomfortable. They should be funky enough to be cool but not so different that they stick out and take away from the rest of your outfit—and they should be exceedingly comfortable (or else, unlike most women, you're never going to wear your uncomfortable dress shoes).

I own a pair of Asics cross-trainers, a black pair of boots from Kenneth Cole, and a brown pair of designer shoes from Donald J. Pliner.

Now I know what you're thinking. "Designer shoes? I deliver pizza." You're right, designer shoes *are* expensive, but expensive shoes are not a waste of your money. I've had my Kenneth Coles for three years. I've worn them almost every day, and they still look new. In contrast, I would have gone through six to ten pairs of Payless shoes in that same amount of time. (I know, because I've done it.) In effect, I actually saved money by buying my boots. The lesson to be learned is that *you can spend*

Black vs. Brown. Why does it always have to be racial with you?

Something many guys never come to understand is that certain outfits do *not* go with black dress shoes. Anytime you're wearing brown or tan, your outfit is begging for a brown dress shoe. If you wear black ones, women will notice (not in a good way). They also notice if your shoes don't match your belt, so make sure that if you're wearing brown shoes, you're also rocking a brown belt. If you have no idea whether to go brown or black, then ask your sister or your mom (or, if desperate, God) for some help. You'll start to get the hang of color combining once someone teaches you a few key pointers.

less money by investing in quality clothing. People who waste money on clothing are people who own *way* more than they wear, or, in other words, most women.

Any other pair of shoes that you own besides your four core pairs is up to you. I own stolen bowling shoes (for leisure), hiking boots, black-and-white-checkered Vans (in honor of legendary movie character Jeff Spicoli), flip-flops, and multicolored suede shoes.

Now let's go underneath it all, to . . .

Underwear

There's nothing I like more than picturing young dudes in their underwear. . . . Oh shit, did I say that out loud? What I mean is, hopefully, eventually, in due time, a girl is going to see you in just your underwear (before they come off), so you should probably make sure that they look good on you.

Tighty-Whities

The overview: Wearing briefs (tighty-whities) is a risky move. Yes, they can give you a certain amount of sex appeal because of the way they cling to you, but I think they're too constricting. I don't know why anyone would want their dick and balls bunched up all day like prisoners of war.

Colin says: Old men, not virile young bucks such as yourself, wear briefs.

Boxers

The overview: From the time I started wearing underwear until eighth grade I wore tighty-whities. In eighth grade I found out about boxers. They were a little weird

Ladies,

Is there anything worse than seeing a guy in an old, hole-ridden, dirty pair of briefs?

at first, seeing as my twig and berries were used to being caged up all day, but I grew to love them. I felt freer and more ventilated.

Colin says: Boxers are a solid choice.

Commando (Free-Ballin')

The overview: Going commando means wearing *no* underwear. I used to be a busboy at a restaurant that will remain nameless (so as to not give it a shred of advertisement). At the restaurant, I was "managed" by a man named Randy who had a peculiar habit. He would stand at the counter where the food came out, to make sure the orders were correct. As he was standing there, he would stick his leg out to the side and shake his foot back and forth on the ground as if he were putting out a cigarette. Could just be a nervous twitch, right? That's what I thought until I heard the sound he made while fidgeting: "OOOOOO!"

It took me a while to realize that Randy's balls were stuck to his leg. He was trying to unstick his sack by shaking his leg out to the side.

Randy was going commando.

Randy probably thought he was super-sexy, keeping his boys out there dangling in the wind. But the truth was, he sounded like an ape, and his scrote undoubtedly smelled like a carload of dirty buttholes at day's end.

Doesn't seem like Randy would be appealing to the ladies, does it?

When you go commando and bare-ball it, you are also taking a serious risk. You're letting your penis bob around right in front of your metal zipper. Sharp metal meeting sensitive skin? Not pretty.

Say you go to the bathroom. You zip up and you accidentally get a tiny bit of your dick caught in the zipper. Ouch! It's happened to me, folks (and I never went commando, ever again). I can't even talk about it anymore; it's making me sick to my stomach. Colin says: Without underwear to create a nice cool environment, you are prone to developing ball stink. Ball stink, plus balls sticking to your leg, plus potential danger with the zipper is enough to leave this Boy Scout commandoless. Just say no to no underwear.

Boxer Briefs

The overview: Boxer briefs are perhaps the end to all of our worries (the ones that are about ample room in the crotch area, that is). Boxer briefs give you the sex appeal of briefs, while maintaining the comfort of boxers. They're good for working out, dates, and pretty much every situation. They're also perfect for guys who can't get used to the free feeling of regular boxers.

Colin says: Boxer briefs may cost a little more, but they're the ticket to a good balance.

You are now schooled in the science of dressing well. That is, considering you've checked your clothing thoroughly for stains, odors, and an excess of wrinkles. Remember, you can vary your style to suit your personality, but one thing is *never* attractive: sloppiness. Your clothes speak for you, so make sure they speak well.

To close out the clothing section I would like to give you one last tip: Leave your hat at home every once in a while. Women want to see your face. And don't show up unshaven when you know you are going to be spending time with a girl. Women like you to look clean and well put together. Or, in the words of my grandfather, "They want you to look sharp, kid."

Casey Sullivan

My friend Casey is a music snob. He swears that, much like your choice in clothing, as a Ladies' Man, your musical taste must be appealing to women and communicate something to them about who you are.

I don't like to admit it, but the dickhead might be on to something here.

You'll play music when the girl of your dreams comes over to your house, you'll play it when you get it on (the wild-monkey dance *can* be accompanied by rhythmic melodies), you'll play it in the car on your dates, and you'll play it during the candlelit dinner that you prepared for the lucky lady. (Don't freak out. I'll show you how to cook in a second.)

Why is musical taste so important? Check this out:

You meet a girl, you're playing it cool, you've got your style in check, your balls aren't sticking to your leg, you ask her out on a date, and she says yes.

Things are going great.

You go to her house to pick her up, you bring her a little present, escort her to the car, open her door like a gentleman, and hop in the driver's seat to start your date.

As soon as you turn the key to start the engine, the power in your car kicks in and your CD player starts to blast the song you were listening to on the drive over. . . .

Ladies,

Why must you all gleefully sing along to Nate Dogg's verse on Snoop Dogg's song, "Ain't No Fun (If the Homies Can't Have None)" when it comes on at a party? Do you realize how ridiculous you all look dancing around, smiling and singing the following lyrics?

When I met you last night baby
Before you opened up your gap
I had respect for ya lady
But now I take it all back
'Cause you gave me all your pussy
And ya even licked my balls
Leave your number on the cabinet
And I promise baby, I'll give ya a call
Next time I'm feelin' kinda horny
You can come on over, and I'll break you off
And if you can't fuck that day, baby
Just lay back, and open your mouth

Think about it the next time you're referring to your vagina as a "gap" or melodically yelling, " 'Cause you gave me all your pussy . . . and you even licked my balls!"

"BITCHES AIN'T SHIT BUT HOS AND SLUTS."
"BITCHES AIN'T SHIT BUT HOS AND SLUTS."

Gentlemen, we have a situation on our hands. You've just boned yourself in the poop-chute.

What is this woman going to think of you now? You have basically taken a metaphorical dump on her entire gender.

Now let's say she *doesn't* think anything of your musical taste. You've got an even bigger problem on your hands: *You're dating a complete moron.*

First and foremost, a true Ladies' Man loves women and would never listen to a song that depicts them so poorly.

Second, in many ways, you are what you listen to. If you listen to garbage that has no meaning, or garbage that has a very disturbing meaning, then that's what you are: disturbing garbage with no meaning. This is why your music should be carefully chosen to reflect your Ladies' Man personality—just like your actions, your words, and your clothes.

I am going to give you some musical suggestions in a second, but keep in mind that you should *listen* to the music you listen to. Don't just hear the songs that are on the radio or MTV. Listen to music that *means* something to you.

If it means something to you, you can't go wrong with the ladies. You're using music as an expression of your heart. And if your heart is telling you that "bitches ain't shit but ho's and sluts," then close this book right now, because you will never, ever be a true Ladies' Man.

As Talib Kweli, a prolific MC, once said, "I never disrespect my women, 'cause I love my mama."

Musical Suggestions

I can't tell you what music will work for *you*. Musical taste is specific to the individual. In effect, only *you* can pick the music that's right for *you*. However, I wanted to give you a place to start from.

I have broken up my musical suggestions into two categories. Category number one consists of music that men and women can usually enjoy together. Category number two is rock music that you don't really want to throw in when you're trying to relax and get to know a girl. (However, some women will enjoy music from this section in a nonromantic environment as well.)

These are just general guidelines. Do your own research before you decide to buy or play anything.

Category 1: Music for a Ladies' Man *and* His Woman

Tori Amos

Fiona Apple (*Tidal*)

*Erykah Badu (*Baduizm*)

Buena Vista Social Club

*Coldplay (*Parachutes, A Rush of Blood to the Head*)

*John Coltrane (*A Love Supreme, Giant Steps, Blue Train*)

*D'Angelo (*Brown Sugar*)

*Miles Davis (*Kind of Blue, Love Songs*)

*Death Cab for Cutie (*We Have the Facts and We're Voting Yes*)

Ella Fitzgerald & Louie Armstrong (*Best of Ella Fitzgerald & Louis Armstrong*)

*Marvin Gaye (*Let's Get It On*)

Lauryn Hill (*The Miseducation of Lauryn Hill*)

*Jets to Brazil (*Orange Rhyming Dictionary*)

Jack Johnson (*Brushfire Fairytales, On and On*)

*Norah Jones (*Come Away with Me*)

Alicia Keys (*Songs in A-minor*)

Bob Marley (*Greatest Hits*)

Dave Matthews Band (*Crash*)

*Maxwell (*Maxwell's Urban Hang Suite, Unplugged*)

*Charles Mingus (*Ah Um*)

Mos Def (*Black on Both Sides*)

Pearl Jam (*Seattle, Washington, November 6, 2000*)

A Perfect Circle
Radiohead (*Kid A, Amnesiac*)
Red Hot Chili Peppers (*Blood Sugar Sex Magik,*
   Californication)
The Roots (*Things Fall Apart*)
*Sade
Santana
Nina Simone
Sonic Youth (*EVOL*)

Category 2: Music for a Ladies' Man to Enjoy Solo

At the Drive-In
Bad Brains
James Brown
Clutch
Deftones
Foo Fighters (*The Color and the Shape*)
Jimi Hendrix
John Lee Hooker
Robert Johnson (*The Complete Recordings*)
The Mars Volta
Nirvana
Radiohead (*The Bends, OK Computer*)
Rage Against the Machine
Tool
Weezer (*Pinkerton, The Blue Album*)

Key:

*   = Good for hookups
( ) = These are the only albums by this artist that are
recommended

Iron Chef

Most women don't expect a man to be able to do much more in the kitchen than microwave a burrito (which my dad has mastered).

When girls find out that you know how to cook, they'll want to try your cooking. For all you slow readers, let me translate: That means *you can get girls to come over to your house.*

You want to learn how to cook? (I'm sure you do now.) Do what I did. Ask your mom (or your dad, if he cooks) to teach you how to make one of your favorite meals. Pay attention while she's teaching you and then practice making the meal a few times before you try it out with your date. Another way to learn is to buy yourself a cookbook and pick out some of the things you would like to try. Again, don't be afraid to ask your mom for help (or ask Iron Chef Masaharu Morimoto, if you know him). If there is no mom or dad in your life, then turn on the cooking channel. Keep it simple when you start out. Don't get too crazy and try to cook stuffed aardvark *en croute* with a peppercorn sauce. Pick some easy recipes to start out with.

There are certain basics you'll learn about cooking when you start: when to use oil, when to use butter, certain ways to make universal sauces, and what heat to cook at. Once you know these techniques and basic rules, you can apply them to any meal you cook. It's like learning how to make a layup in basketball: Once you get the fundamentals of making the layup, then you can improvise.

I am going to include a recipe for a meal to get you started. Keep in mind that guys who cook are sexy and impressive to women—and a dying breed of male in our fast-food nation.

Learn it.
Know it.
Live it.

A Recipe for a Ladies' Man and His Woman

Chicken Piccata with Capers

This dish can be prepared in forty-five minutes.

You will need (for the main course):
A ¾-pound whole skinless, boneless chicken breast
1 tablespoon vegetable oil
2 tablespoons unsalted butter
2 tablespoons dry white wine
1 tablespoon fresh lemon juice
3 tablespoons minced fresh parsley leaves
1 tablespoon drained bottled capers (chopped)
flour, salt, pepper, and paprika

You will also need (for the rice and salad):
A bag of brown or white rice (your choice)
A head of lettuce (any lettuce other than iceberg)
A tomato
A cucumber
Salad dressing (your choice)

So you've got your ingredients, and, for the first time in your life, you've uncovered the great mystery of the difference between the teaspoon and the tablespoon (and you only had to ask your mom twice). Congratulations! Now I know at this point in the evening, with all of the ingredients sprawled out in front of you in the kitchen, you're probably tempted to pop open the wine and get shitfaced. Understandable. But take it from somebody who's been down that road: When your date walks in and finds you unconscious on the floor, with raw chicken breasts and vegetable oil coating your naked body, you're probably not going to get a good-night kiss (or a second chance).

Before you start preparing the chicken, you should start cooking the rice. Rice takes a decent amount of time to cook, so it's always better to start it early. Check the bag of rice for cooking directions. (It ain't rocket science.) I suggest brown rice, but if you're in love with white rice, then have it your way. And don't make instant rice! Instant rice is disgusting.

Begin the chicken dish by cutting the chicken breast into two halves with a sharp knife. Then flatten the pieces of chicken between sheets of plastic wrap (or waxed paper). You can flatten the chicken by smashing it with the palm of your hand. The benefits of this are twofold: 1.) tenderization; and 2.) you'll beat out any pent-up sexual tension before your date arrives. Mix a cup of flour with a little salt, pepper, and paprika, and dredge the chicken pieces through this mixture (or put the mixture in a bag and shake the chicken pieces one by one in the bag until they are coated). In a large,

LM

"To taste" means that you should add a little spice, then sample a tiny bit of the sauce to make sure it tastes good. If you think it needs more spice, add a little, and repeat the process until the sauce tastes good to you. Remember: You can always add more spice, but once you *over*spice, you're screwed.

heavy skillet—ask your mom or dad what a skillet is—heat 1 tablespoon each of the butter and the oil over a medium-high heat until the foam subsides. Then place the pieces of chicken in the pan. You will cook the chicken for one minute on each side, or until the breasts are browned. Once browned, put them on an oven-safe platter and into the oven, set at 200 degrees.

Next, pour off the fat from the skillet and add to the skillet your remaining 1 tablespoon of butter, the wine, and the lemon juice, and bring the mixture to a boil. Stir in the capers and the parsley, and add salt and pepper to taste.

Let the sauce reduce until it reaches an appropriate consistency. (Not thin like chicken noodle soup and not thick like gravy but somewhere in between.) When the sauce is done, throw the chicken into the skillet for approximately five minutes to fully cook the meat. Then remove the breasts and spoon the sauce over the meat.

You can prepare a fresh, simple salad, using the ingredients listed above, a few minutes before the chicken and rice are ready. Most women love salad.

Enjoy.

• • •

Okay, so you've got some cool music to check out and share with the ladies in your life, a recipe to make a nice meal for your future girl, your clothing options have been expanded, and your balls aren't parading around (unwrapped) on the inside of your pants. Just relax and give yourself some time to let all that advice sink in. You'll be refining your style for the rest of your life; just be glad that you have a solid start. You're already ten times more attractive than you were when you started this book. Dude, you're on your way to becoming *the total package*.

But first, we need to deal with some issues you may need to address about *you*. The way you look, the way you're built. Basically, we need to talk about your dick.

Don't worry; this won't hurt a bit. . . .

Ladies,

If you have a guy friend who is clueless about style, then help him out. Go shopping with him for clothes that women will appreciate. Encourage him to get a nice haircut. Teach him how to style his hair—for God's sake, I had my hair parted down the middle for eighteen years of my life and nobody said *anything!*

❷
Your Penis and You

"See, the problem is that God gives men a brain and a
penis, and only enough blood to run one at a time."
—ROBIN WILLIAMS

In the end, there is no doubt about the most important
body image issue for guys: our dicks. Sure, height,
weight, muscle tone, and many other body issues exist,
but nothing comes within an expanding universe's
length of our dick's importance to self-image. You could
be chunky, short, and have little to no muscle tone, but if
you are confident about the size, shape, and appearance
of your penis, then you feel like Jennifer Lopez facing off
against Avril Lavigne in a "Who's got a bigger ass?" con-
test. (Note to readers: If you really do feel like J.Lo on a

daily basis, you may be a woman trapped in a man's body.)

But who among us is really confident about his dick (besides me)? A show of hands indicates, not many of you. So before going on, take a deep breath and let go of all the worries that you've carried around in relation to your penis.

Your dick is good enough.

Your dick is smart enough.

And gosh darn it, people will like your dick.

I used to be terrified about whether or not my dick was "normal." I worried that it was too short. I worried that is was too thin. I worried about my juvenile, peach-fuzz pubic hair. I even worried that my balls weren't big enough. And, really, who cares about the size of their balls?

I was so scared I was abnormal that I wouldn't even take a pee in the stand-up urinals—for fear of another guy seeing my penis and thinking I was some sort of freak. I only used bathroom stalls (with the door locked). In short, I worried about my penis daily and was in constant trepidation of a guy shaming me or a girl laughing at me—because I knew there would come a day when a girl would see my penis (and maybe even play with it).

I want you to know that you have nothing to worry about. Your dick is normal, and your dick (or lack thereof) will get the job done sexually (more on this later). But, more important, your dick, and the proper amount of lubricant, will always satisfy *you*.

My Friend Dick

Don't worry, this section doesn't have a ridiculous title like What's Going On in Your Pants. I also won't be referring to your penis as a "reproductive organ" or "your manhood." I can't tell you how much garbage I've read in which people use these terms.

It's a dick.

So, hey, let's call a dick a dick.

Or Richard.

Or even Mushroom Tip Rich, but not a "male reproductive organ."

Richard is quite an important instrument to guys. The question it always comes down to is . . .

"Is My Dick Big or Small?"

Your dick is small.

But don't worry; we've done very scientific studies and found that the more copies of this book a guy buys, the bigger his dick gets. Yes, *it actually makes your dick bigger when you read this book.*

All right, maybe that's bullshit, but it would be a great marketing technique.

The reason we don't know where our dicks fall in the penis-size continuum is because we're so uncomfortable seeing other guys naked that we don't know what *their* dicks look like in relation to ours.

Most of the guys on my high-school basketball team—come to think of it, *all* of them—didn't shower in the locker room after games. We were all too embarrassed to be naked in front of other guys.

Which I've found is the case for most of us.

We have no real basis upon which to judge whether our dicks are "normal." And there's no way in hell we're going to ask another guy how big *his* dick is, because then *he will think we are gay.* (Note: There is nothing wrong with being gay.) To make matters worse, if you watch the occasional porno, you're bound to feel like you were absent the day they gave out dicks the size of tree trunks. So what's the *real* deal?

The truth is that there is no "normal" dick. I've seen my fair share of Richards in locker rooms since high school, and I can tell you with confidence that they all look different.

Different length.

Different width.

Different tip.

Different color.

Different balls. (Although balls all have one striking similarity: They're the only body part that comes out of the womb looking a hundred years old.)

I'm sure some of you are uncomfortable knowing that I've seen other guys' dicks in locker rooms. Many of you, like me at one point, probably do everything you can to avoid catching a glimpse of somebody's package. I guess I've reached a point where it doesn't threaten my manhood to walk by a person and *not* do a 180 to avoid it. We're all curious; it's just hard for us to admit it.

And don't pretend for one damn second that you've never taken a look at someone else's dick while you were at the urinal. I know you have. Because we *all* have. You get curious to know if your dick is normal, so you shoot over a quick glance at the guy peeing next to you. It's all right. You can admit it now. No one will judge.

And don't worry; this doesn't make you gay. (Although you *could* be gay and do it, it's just that you wouldn't be gay *because* you did it.)

Average Dick Size

So where *does* your package fall on the penis-size continuum? From the info that I have gathered in my career as

a man, I have determined that an average-sized dick is
about . . .

twelve inches.

Don't worry. I'm just messing with you. For real, the
average dick is between five and six inches when it's
hard. You may have a larger one; you may have a smaller
one. That doesn't make your dick any better or worse
than the next guy's.

I know some girls who prefer smaller dicks and some
girls who prefer larger dicks. Some who prefer thicker
and some who prefer thinner. Some who prefer brown
and some who prefer black.

You get the picture: It doesn't matter how big or
small your dick is. Girls just want to feel like you're comfortable with your body. They want to feel your *confidence*. So stay confident.

Besides, if you're worried about satisfying a girl, you
should know that it has nothing to do with size. It
doesn't even have to do with your dick. You could be
completely dickless and still satisfy a woman sexually.

How, you ask? One hint: It's rolling around inside
your mouth.

The fact is, there isn't a sane woman in the world who
would rather be penetrated by a man's huge penis than
helped to have an orgasm by his adept tongue. (But I'm
getting ahead of myself. All this will all be covered later,
in part three.)

So what have we learned so far?

Women are not men. (This may seem obvious, but
stay with me.) While an average guy will like a girl just
because she's got a hot body, a girl isn't going to like you
just because you have a huge penis. In fact, chances are
that she won't even want to see your penis until she's already decided that she likes you in the first place. A

woman will like you because you're intelligent, funny, a smart dresser, a great lover—none of which has to do with the size of your dick.

So say it with me: The size of your penis does *not* matter. What *does* matter is that you accept your body and that you learn how to use it to please a woman.

Now take a deep breath.

Relax.

Your dick is just fine the way it is.

Love your dick.

I think that's the title of a new self-help book. . . .

Love Your Dick, by Colin Mortensen-Sánchez.

Tricks That Dick Can Do

Now, bear in mind that I said, "Love your dick." I never said, "Trust your dick," because trusting your penis would be a grave, grave mistake.

The penis, in fact, is the most *un*trustworthy appendage on your body. Unlike, say, your arm or your leg, which will do exactly what you tell them, your penis has a mind of its own.

Shrinkage

Shrinkage seems to occur for no reason at all and at the most inopportune times. (I suspect this is our karmic payback for being able to pee standing up.) You take a cold shower, come out all clean and refreshed, and your dick has taken on the size and shape of a piece of baby corn. I'm talking tiny. Your balls are wound up so tight that they've become one ball instead of two.

Shrinkage.

Why do one's dick and balls become so small when they get cold? A simple reason, really: survival. Shrinkage happens in order to assure that your boys don't get *too* cold, which can kill sperm and leave your balls open to nasty things like frostbite. By drawing in closer to your body, your dick and balls assure their relative warmth, and the health of your semen.

Under normal circumstances I wouldn't care about shrinkage, because it doesn't matter what my dick looks like. But if you're lucky, there will be occasions when a *girl* will be looking at your dick. For that reason, you have to understand how to control and conceal your shrinkage.

Why? Because most women don't know the extent to which a penis's size can vary (with or without shrinkage). They don't understand that sometimes your penis is just a hell of a lot smaller than its potential.

I polled as many women as I could concerning dick size, and the large majority figured that a dick only fluctuates about one inch from the "limp" state to the "hard" state. I don't know about you guys, but I have a lot more range. By the logic of the women polled, if your dick is six inches when it's hard, then it's going to be five inches when it's soft. Not true. Not even close to true.

I would say that a penis can fluctuate by at least 50 percent of its hard size at any given moment (not taking shrinkage into account). This means that a six-inch dick can get at least as small as three inches for no reason at all. And with shrinkage I believe it can fluctuate up to 80 or 90 percent of its hard length, meaning that a six-inch erect penis can get as small as one inch during shrinkage.

Stay with me here.

If a girl thinks that your dick only varies about one inch between the hard and limp stages and she catches you coming out of a cold shower with a one-inch soft penis, then she's going to think you have a two-inch dick!

We can't blame women for this. They don't have

dicks. Why should they know? The point is that it's our job to never let a woman catch us during our shrinkage times, and for that matter, to avoid letting women see us in most limp states.

Sure, in the grand scheme of things the size of your dick doesn't matter, but nothing positive can come of a woman thinking you have a half-inch penis when it's really capable of five or six hard inches.

Semis

Besides a boner, a "semi" is the only state in which you should allow a girl to see Richard. A semi is the state when your dick is in between limp and hard. You can still squeeze it, so it's not completely hard, but it's fuller than a limp dick.

The story I am about to tell has nothing to do with me, but I'll tell it in the first person because stories work better that way.

My friends and I decided to rent a cabin in Lake Tahoe for a week during the summertime. We had fourteen people up there. Half girls. Half guys. (Hooking up works out better when there's an even number of guys and girls. If the numbers are uneven, someone inevitably ends up having to watch, and that can get real ugly.) We're at the lake, and someone decides that we should all go skinny-dipping.

There was a private cove close to our cabin. No one outside our group would even know we were there.

The good news: It was a full moon out, so we would be able to see the ladies perfectly.

The bad news: It was a full moon out, so the ladies would be able to see *us* perfectly.

First thing that runs through my head: "Great, these girls are going to be staring at my limp penis."

Then, a lightbulb: I'll just chum it up. I'll fluff the little guy. I'll make sure I have a semi before I jump in the water. Then I'll make sure to be the first *out* of the lake and into a towel. That way the girls won't see my shrink-a-fied dick.

We get to the cove wearing only sandals and our bathing suits. All the guys go behind one tree to take off their trunks, and the girls go behind another to change out of their swimsuits. I turn to the guys and let them in on my plan.

"I'm not crazy, I'm gonna go chum it up behind a bush (they just stare at me, no reaction). You know, just stroke it or tug on it a bit until it's a semi."

This puts them all in a difficult position. After all, if I go out with a semi and they go out with shrinkage, reputations are going to suffer. If some of them join in on my chumming plan, will the non-chummers tell the girls we gave it the old chummeroosky?

Without another word I leave and position myself behind a bush.

One by one they all casually walk away to their own bushes.

What a sight: all seven of us rapidly tugging, behind shrubbery barely covering our asses, trying to get semis before the girls change.

Our dicks are in ready position, and the girls are waiting for us down by the water. We all come running out from behind the tree, huge semis flopping in the wind, grins from ear to ear, screaming at the top of our lungs, without a care in the world.

It was a beautiful moment.

E.T. Bone Home

While it's never negative for your penis to be in a semi state of mind, the arrival of an unexpected and uninvited boner can put a damper on any occasion.

An Unexpected Boner Drops By for a Visit

Scientists discovered that a man's beard grows faster the more he thinks about sex (due to increased levels of testosterone). And since my facial hair proliferates exponentially by the day, I can tell you that the majority of unexpected boners arrive when your mind wanders off into the sexual realm—which, for most of us, is the realm where our minds rest for 80 to 90 percent of our lives.

While writing this passage, my mind just traveled to an ancient carboniferous forest filled with giant naked women. It wasn't by choice. Hell, I'm trying to write about uninvited hard dicks, and my brain found a way to order blood to my penis by creating images of inordinately large, nude Amazonian beauties. I took a few minutes to decide where I wanted this paragraph to go and ended up in a sexual wonderland. Hence, I am sitting at the computer with an uninvited boner telling myself to focus so that I can meet my deadline for writing about unexpected boners.

In short, a boner can come at just about any time for just about any reason.

You have to salute your penis, because even though it's only required to handle two main bodily functions (peeing and expelling semen), it accomplishes those two tasks *really well*. Any guy named Colin who has ever wet his bed as a grown man—or ended up masturbating in a public bathroom stall while laying over at an international airport—knows this all too well. For the majority of a man's life, his penis outsmarts his brain.

This is no small accomplishment.

You're in class, and your brain is trying to absorb the complexity of algebra, but your dick points you in the direction of the hottest girl in the room. Once there, you notice that she's wearing a skirt, and so you picture what it would be like if she weren't wearing a skirt. Then you picture her over at your house, in your bed, when your parents aren't home.

And all of a sudden, you've got a rock-hard boner in math class.

When this happens, I think you need to thank your penis for having done what it thought needed to be done (after all, it's only trying to help), and then bring your focus back to algebra. You may have to do this five or six thousand times a day during your teenage years, but you can reduce that number to a low three to four thousand times a day by the time you are in your twenties. If you do not learn how to let go of your sexual fantasies when you need to focus on productive matters, like school or work, then you will never accomplish anything.

And keep in mind that someday soon (hopefully), you will be hooking up with a girl, honoring the ease with which your soft penis turns into a boner.

There are times when a boner is welcome, but when it is not, picture your grandmother doing the splits in a two-piece bathing suit.

Let go of boner-inducing thoughts.

But when you can't, you should think about:

The Tuck-Under Method

The tuck-under-method is a time-tested (by me) response to the wayward penis. It can be put into effect at any point in time, in response to any boner. Let's start with the math class situation.

You get an unexpected hard-on. You're trying to convince it to go away without a fight when . . . the bell rings. Let's assume that you don't want all the kids in school to think that *math really turns you on*. You need a way out . . . and fast.

Sounds like you're in desperate need of the tuck-under method, my friend.

What is the tuck-under method?

That is a question that has been proposed for centuries by the wisest philosophers; Plato, Confucius, Marx, Alcott, Foucault, Socrates, Nietzsche, even Gandhi, have all attempted to pontificate upon the tuck-under method, but to no avail. I will succeed where they have failed.

The tuck-under method is when you adjust your penis so that it is being held vertically against your stomach by your pants. Or shorts. You hold it in place by trapping it in between the waistband of your pants and your stomach.

Why is the TUM so ingenious?

The physics involved are what make the TUM so revolutionary. Your waistband will hold your boner up until it gets limp again. Once it gets limp, it will fall back into place. And you won't care that it fell back into place, because it won't be hard anymore.

Furthermore, you can go on with your life after tucking it under, and no one will know the difference between your stomach and your boner. Nothing will be prodding or protruding from your pants.

Tuck, Tuck, Goose

There are two ways to get your penis into the tuck-under position. First, by inconspicuously sticking your hand in your pants and flipping it up against your stomach. To do this you have to be very careful. You don't want anyone in the vicinity (especially a girl) to catch you with your hand down your pants.

If they think you're playing with yourself, that could hurt your chances. Not only with the girl who's watching you touch your hard dick in public, but with *every woman she knows*. However, if someone *does* see you adjusting, then make a manly, slightly annoyed facial expression—as if you just didn't like where your dick was resting and needed to shift.

Act cool.

The second, and more socially acceptable way to get your dick into the tuck-under position is to do it *outside* of your pants. If your dick is hard and leaning to one side, you can pull the waist of your pants out a bit and coax your dick into flipping up against your stomach. All the while, your shirt is covering the rush of blood to the head that lies under the surface.

If you *can* do it like this, do it. Nothing bad can happen if she sees you regulating outside of your pants (as long as you appear manly while doing it). Think of baseball players. They adjust themselves all the time. Act indifferent, and again, use that "What's this doing here?" expression while adjusting. Play it cool; it's the easy way out of any potentially embarrassing situation.

Why TUM?

The beauty of the TUM is that it's undetectable. It's like the stealth bomber of boners. (Except for the fact that the TUM can't really kill anyone and doesn't cost billions in tax dollars.)

The TUM is not solely to be used at school. I use the TUM every time I get a public boner. You can use it at a club, or even in a public park.

Wherever you are—tuck it under.

Do you have a boner as lunch ends and need to walk all the way across campus for your next class?

Tuck it under.

Are you miniature golfing on a date and feeling a boner coming on as she bends over and scoops up both of your balls from the hole?

Tuck it under.

I can't say enough about tucking it under, because it's

been an absolute lifesaver for me. However, beware of the TUM when you don't have a shirt on.

When you do the shirtless tuck-under, the penis tip can be seen due to the fact that it is being held in place by your waistband. If you don't have a shirt on and you go for the TUM, it can be potentially devastating to innocent bystanders. Unsuspecting folks who glance at your waist will get a glimpse of the mushroom tip. That can be scary as hell coming out of nowhere. You could scar someone for life. The TUM is *not* recommended for times when you are shirtless.

Mangina

I was explaining the TUM to my friends Jesse and Kim because they were oblivious to it. (In retrospect I should have just held out and made them buy the book.) Anyway, Jesse nodded as if he understood what the tuck-under method was, but I could tell he was having a little trouble grasping the concept.

Meanwhile, I notice a "What in God's name are you talking about?" look cross Kim's face. So I ask her,

"What's wrong with the tuck-under method?"

"Well, it just seems like it's a bit uncomfortable."

"Uncomfortable? It's perfectly comfy."

I proceed to explain that your boner rests right there against your stomach and your waistline.

Kim bursts into laughter.

A look of recognition crosses Jesse's face.

Kim then comments, "I thought you were talking about tucking it *under,* as in pulling it around the backside."

"Pulling it around the backside?!"

She'd thought I was talking about the *mangina*!

If you don't know what the mangina is, then you're about to get book-learned. The mangina occurs when you trap your penis behind your legs and it looks like you have a vagina (without the opening). You stand there with your knees touching, and it looks like you don't have a penis. Just a bush. (Don't act like you're above this, because we've all looked in the mirror to see what the mangina looks like. We *all* want to know what it looks like to be dickless.)

If you were under the same impression as Kim was, then I urge you to *reread* my description of the application of the TUM. The last thing I want is for some guy to give himself a mangina at school, at a dance, or anytime he gets a boner. Can you imagine the girl you're dancing with watching as you try to tuck your hard penis behind your legs and in between your ass cheeks? I'm pretty sure that's a deal-breaker.

Ladies,

Every guy I know has applied the mangina to himself at one time or another, which is proof positive that men have vagina envy. I guess Freud's sexist ass never analyzed the time he spent naked in front of the mirror with his dick tucked in between his inner thighs and his ass cheeks.

Other *Dick*issues

Aside from your penis staging a mutiny and acting out every once in a while, there are other ways it can cause you stress. Maybe there are things about it that are just *different* from other guys' and you don't know how to feel about that. For example . . .

Circumcised vs. Uncircumcised

I'm going to make this real easy. It doesn't matter if you're rockin' the hoodie or not. Love your dick. From what I understand, the majority of males born these days are not getting circumcised. That statistic doesn't mean much, unless you are one of the idiots who makes fun of uncircumcised kids. In that case, prepare to be made fun of yourself in a few years.

If your penis is uncircumcised, you'll have to do a little extra work to keep it clean. Other than that, you're no different than the rest of us.

U-Turn Peter

The U-turn peter is a dick that curves to one side. Yes, it's completely normal. Don't worry about it; lots of people have dicks like this. It does not make you a freak, and it will not in any way inhibit your ability to have sex.*

*_Warning:_ Certain guys have penis issues that make it hard, if not impossible, to have intercourse. Some of the issues, such as having a penis that curves 60 degrees to the right or left when hard, can be cured through successful surgery. If you think you have a serious issue with your dick, then you should tell your parents and see a doctor as soon as possible.

How Do You Spell _Penis_ in Braille?

Some guys have tiny bumps around the heads of their penises. If your doctor has taken a look at these bumps and told you they are nothing to be concerned about, then _don't be concerned about them._ (Especially if you are a virgin.) This is a completely normal phenomenon called "penile papules." These papules will not inhibit your ability to use your penis in any way.

Dick's Friends, Balls

As we've already discussed, your balls are some pretty homely little guys.

But how can you tell if they're normal? Answer: It's pretty hard.

I was talking to one of my friends on the phone just the other day, and out of nowhere he told me that he was going to get his balls tested for cancer.

"Why? What's wrong with them?" I responded.

"I don't know, one of my balls feels round and solid, like a ball, and the other one feels like it has this extra sort of cartilage attached to it."

"*Oh, that*. Yeah, I have that too. . . . I think a lot of guys have that, dude. It's totally normal."

"Really? Whew," he exhales.

Now I'm not saying you shouldn't check your balls out if you think something is wrong with them. Medical advice about the testes is always a good idea. But the strange part of this conversation is that my friend and I had been close for over a decade—and this subject had never been brought up by either one of us.

Guys obviously don't realize that they're not alone when it comes to body issues. We all have similar experiences. At twenty-one years old my friend finally found out that he was normal and that this deal with his balls was pretty average. But for all that time, he'd worried alone. You shouldn't have to live with something like that for so long. If you have a good friend, talk to him about your questions and concerns. And be an encouraging listener in return. This can help you deal with your problems and insecurities. (Women know this. That's why they're so much more in tune with each other than we are.)

You shouldn't just take your friends' advice when it comes to medical issues. You should see a doctor if you have questions or concerns. However, it doesn't hurt to see if other guys are going through the same things you are.

Testicle "Experts"

Before writing this book, I researched the market to see what was out there for guys like us to read. Several of the books I read included a "ball-o-meter" to measure your balls.

I'm not kidding. I don't know what they called it for real (it certainly wasn't "ball-o-meter"). Basically, it was an outline of a pair of "typical" testes so readers could see how they measured up. Let's get one thing straight right now: *I don't want you plastering your balls to my book.* I know you own the book and everything, but for God's sake, have some dignity.

Ladies,
    Can you imagine reading a book that encouraged you to slap your labia majora on the page to determine whether or not you were coming along appropriately?

Masturbation

> "Having sex is like playing bridge. If you don't have a
> good partner, you'd better have a good hand."
> —WOODY ALLEN

Okay, so we've talked at length about the trouble your penis can cause. Now let's talk about the pleasure it can give you. That's right, I'm talking about shaking hands with Richard.

Masturbation.

I am going to share a piece of information with you about the first time I masturbated.

Information that I've never doled out to anybody in the free world. It's a skeleton that I still can't believe is in my closet. A secret so piteous that my friends and loved ones will be forced to use it against me for life. (Oh wait, my friends are illiterate morons! Except for one of you. You know who you are.)

Deep breath in, and release. . . .

I first masturbated while watching *Family Feud*.

Yes, that's right; I first spanked it while viewing a popular game show that features great-grannies and their extended relatives battling it out for cash and prizes.

Now, if you are a sane person with a functioning brain, then you are thinking, "Why? Why would Colin have decided to masturbate for the first time in his life while watching the *Feud*?" This is a valid question.

I was alone on the couch—in the summer between ninth and tenth grade—watching television. In my mind, I was replaying a conversation that I had recently had with my best friend. We had been talking about girls that we wanted to hook up with when our banter had taken an unexpected turn.

Best Friend: "Yeah, I always picture Tonya when I masturbate."

I had spent most of that school year (ninth grade) in New York, and my friend and I had recently reunited in California. Apparently, many things had gone down since my departure.

Young Colin: "You've masturbated before?"

Best Friend: "Yeah. Pretty much everyone that I know masturbates. At least everyone on the baseball team. Guys are always making jokes about it at practice. I heard them talking about it, so I tried it."

Young Colin: "Wow."

Best Friend: "You've never done it? Ever?"

Young Colin: "No. I've never really even thought about it. I don't even know how to do it."

Best Friend: "It ain't rocket science."

Young Colin: "Right . . . So . . . you wanna shoot some hoops later?"

Best Friend: "Cool."

I couldn't believe it! I'd left the state for nine months and suddenly my best friend was an avid masturbator who talked about his ejaculatory habits with his buddies during baseball practice? He could've called. Or at least sent a postcard. I had been missing out on valuable masturbation time.

I began to interview other friends (in depth) and

Ladies,
    This was somewhere around the time you were dis-
covering the showerhead, or the dripping faucet, or the
reverberating stereo speaker, or the comfort of your
middle-and-ring-finger combination, or a vibrator.

found out that pretty much every single guy in my ninth-grade class had masturbated. I felt left out.

To this day, I can't believe I never went to scratch below the border, got a little excited, fathomed the possibilities, and got to flogging. I can't believe I never climbed a pole during recess at grade school, realized that the gyration felt good, and proceeded to hump the wood until climax (this is how one of my friends first got off—after that day he was habitually late to return from recess).

I had never even had a wet dream.

Now that I think about it, I probably hadn't thought to masturbate simply because I hadn't had an orgasm (of any kind). And I was nearly in the *tenth grade*. It seemed like I was an extremely late bloomer.

So there I was on the couch, recalling that all of my friends and the entire school (it seemed) had masturbated.

Do you remember when *Family Feud* used to have celebrity feuds and cross-promote other shows on their network? I do. Occasionally they would have the American Gladiators on to battle it out against a handful of soap opera stars. *American Gladiator* was a physical-challenge type of game show that pitted mammoth, hormone-filled "gladiators" against average citizens in grueling events. The gladiators were the most amazing physical specimens I had ever seen. Most of them were male, but a few gladiators were female, and while there was the occasional unattractive Amazonian monster, there was always the strong but feminine female warrior with the body of a goddess.

I was watching the Feud and I had a boner—that same boner would hang around for the entire decade to follow. Back then I could get a hard-on from the smell of a fruit roll-up. So right there on the couch, I decided to undertake one of the most important physical challenges of my life. I took off my shorts and became transfixed with the moments in the *Feud* when my female gladiator companion would jump up and down in celebration of a personal victory. And when she correctly guessed a piece of clothing worn by the Three Musketeers—I believe she said, "A mask?"—I began to masturbate.

Fourteen years of captivation had me ready to detonate. In the blink of an eye, I came all over my hand. And the rug. (Sorry, Dad.)

My left eye twitched for twenty or thirty seconds post-orgasm. I couldn't move. I was paralyzed, and semen was coating my fingers. The texture and sight of come was shocking and a bit of a turn-off. But despite my lack of planning, this worm had finally become a butterfly that day in front of Richard Dawson and the American Gladiators.

From that moment on, nothing in my life would be the same. Once a man feels the sensation of an orgasm and links his joy to women, the next few decades of his life will be characterized by a constant struggle for power between his penis and his brain. Usually this struggle

M or F?

It's a little-spoken-of fact that many heterosexual guys have their first sexual experience with another boy during childhood. It's okay if you are one of these people, and it doesn't mean that you are gay (although you could be). Many straight guys have their first brush with sex with a male friend, and they come out just fine (pun intended).

ends with your dick leading the way and your mind making excuses and creating alibis all along the way.

So there I was, convulsing, and, unexpectedly, I felt guilty. As I walked to the bathroom to undergo the proper cleanup, I swore to myself that I wouldn't tell anyone that I had masturbated. Yes, I had just experienced the greatest ecstasy of my fourteen years on this planet, but at the same time, I felt as if I had done something wrong. I decided that I shouldn't masturbate again.

It was a bad thing to do.

But really, what was wrong with pleasing myself? What was wrong with discovering my own body? What was wrong with tugging one out?

Looking back now, I know that my discomfort was a result of the millions of messages I had received from various well-meaning adults (and organizations) about masturbation.

Little by little, as we grow up, we are taught that we do not have the right to control our own bodies. Many people live their entire lives not feeling entitled to decide what to do with themselves. That's what you call *a load of horseshit*. We should all have the right to treat our bodies with love and respect (regardless of what the world tells us) . . . and pleasing myself sexually turned out to be a great way to relieve stress and to understand my body.

And understanding your own body will only make it easier to understand your girlfriend's body and to communicate your sexual needs to your girl (when the appropriate time comes).

A Few Key Masturbatory Pointers

1. **Use lubricant.** (Any kind of lotion, soap, shampoo, or conditioner will do.) I only advocate going dry

(no lube) in an emergency situation. If you use lubricant, then it's less likely that your dick will get raw or irritated. Lotion, soap, shampoo, and/or conditioner can sometimes irritate the tip of your penis, so if you are scared of possible irritation, then go with a water-based lube. You can also use an all-natural soap, lotion, shampoo, or conditioner if you wish to lessen the possibility of irritating Mushroom Tip Rich.

2. **Always have a "nut-rag" on hand** to catch your semen when you come. A nut-rag can be tissue, toilet paper, or even an old shirt (we've all had to go there).

3. **Find a private and secure place** to get your rocks off. The shower, for example, is a great place to masturbate, because you're (hopefully) never going to get walked in on by a family member. And cleanup is easy in the shower—if you use soap as your lubricant, then technically you're washing and masturbating at the same time. And they say guys are dirty.

4. **Skip the porn.** Looking at pornographic magazines and watching pornographic movies while masturbating is not a good idea. Straight porno usually portrays men in positions of power over women, and the sex is always centered around the man having an orgasm and the woman simply enjoying the man's pleasure. Women seldom get off (come) in pornos, and the sex is hardly ever loving. Give in to the porn, and your first impressions of sex will be unhealthy. Your pleasure should never be equated with a woman putting herself in a degrading position.

5. **Use your imagination.** Instead of porn, I use my mind to create scenarios that turn me on. There is one very important aspect of these scenarios that

I'd like to pass along: You should **always make sure that, in your fantasy, the woman has an orgasm.** Of course you can have an orgasm too, but wait until you have made the woman come in your daydream before the story becomes about your pleasure. This way you are programming yourself to please your woman and to get *turned on* by pleasing your woman. These are both very useful mental practices. You will learn much more about female pleasure in the sex section, but these are some things to keep in mind with regards to masturbation.

Additional Masturbation Facts

Masturbating can (but is not guaranteed to) help you last longer in bed. This is important—especially if you don't have much experience in bed. Masturbating helps you become accustomed to having your penis stimulated, which means that once you get into bed, you won't burst before the party gets started.

Ladies,

When I encourage guys to use their imagination when masturbating, you have to understand that they will be imagining *you*. They'll probably never admit to it, but when you wear that cute outfit to the mall, guys remember it, and they bring that mental picture with them to the shower.

Self-induced orgasms comply with the *law of diminishing returns:* Your first orgasm from masturbation feels the best (and happens the quickest), your second feels the second best (and happens the second quickest), your third the third best, and so on. . . . Sure, there are variables and exceptions to this rule, but more often than not your orgasms get slightly less intense the more you masturbate. Because of this fact, masturbating can ensure that you will last longer when you end up hooking up with a girl (and trust me, you're going to need all the help you can get, or so I've heard).

Post-orgasm pissing is a wild ride. After sex, your pee will try to impress you by doing circus tricks—like shooting two lines of urine in opposite directions, dousing the seat and soaking the floor, or it will flaunt its ability to spray itself all over the bathroom like a showerhead. It's as if your urine wants to show you that it too is important—just as important as its archenemy, semen. You are not weird if it is hard for you to pee after masturbating. It happens to everyone.

Masturbation will not:

- Make you go blind (unless your semen is radioactive, and you shoot your load into your own eye—I guess love really is in the eye of the beholder).

- Give you more zits (there is no relation between masturbation and acne).

- Render you unable to have children later in life.

I've had more sexual encounters with my hand than with any woman on this planet, and the same is currently (or will someday) be true for you. Introduce your hand and your penis to each other, because I can assure you that it will be the beginning of a beautiful and long-lasting relationship.

When Good Jerking Goes Bad

Like anything that feels good, it's possible to engage in *too much* masturbation. Here's how to know when to chill out and stow the monkey in his cage.

1. If masturbation is getting in the way of your daily responsibilities, hobbies, or relationships—like school, work, basketball practice, or your friendships. If your friend asks you if you want to go to the movies and you say, "No thanks man, I plan on jerking off ten times in the next two hours," then you may have a problem.

2. If you find yourself doing it against your own will—if you're masturbating so frequently that it even bothers *you*, then you may have a problem.

3. If your dick is constantly raw or irritated from masturbation, then you're probably doing it too much (or doing it the wrong way).

4. If you are always thinking about it, even after you just masturbated, then you may have a problem. Masturbation shouldn't dominate or negatively affect the quality of your life. Sexual gratification can become an addiction. As with most things in life, moderation is the key.

If you think you're having a problem with masturbation, talk to someone (like a doctor, therapist, or guidance counselor) about it. But also, remember to cut yourself some slack. Because masturbation is fairly new to you, you'll probably be doing it more often than, say, a thirty-year-old man, and you'll probably be experimenting with masturbation more often than, let's say, your father. (Yes, it's true: Your dad masturbates. Go ahead and throw up, then come back to reading.)

Your first orgasm will probably be one of the greatest feelings of your life thus far. So the odds say that you're going to be masturbating quite often. Orgasms are new to you. Enjoy them.

Making the First Move

"This quote is funny and clever."
—COLIN MORTENSEN-SÁNCHEZ

I hear you all out there—whining, complaining, wondering, "Colin, when are you going to stop talking about your freakish masturbatory habits and start teaching us how to hook up with girls?" Have it your way. But first I'll teach you how to interact (successfully) with a member of the opposite sex, which can, in due time, lead to a hookup.

By now, you know yourself a little better, and you're confident in your style. This sets the stage for you to start pursuing girls. But how do you meet them, talk to them, and get them to notice that you're around?

In theory, it's pretty simple: All you need to meet any girl who interests you is an *"in."* What's an in? An in is something the two of you have in common, like a class, a hobby, a church, or anything under the sun. Sometimes ins will present themselves to you, dropping into your lap like a well-paid "dancer" at your friend's birthday party. Other times, you'll have to create them. In either case, when you find an in, you must act on it *immediately*.

Now, I wouldn't normally do this, because in many ways I am ending Monty Python's quest for the Holy Grail, but you know, I kinda like you, so I'm going to divulge to you the three best manufactured ins I've come across in my time. Please treat them with the respect and dignity that they deserve.

The First "In"

PEZ!

That's right, good old-fashioned Pez. You're at a party, or a dance, or the beach, or anywhere you see a girl you want to meet, but you don't have an in. What do you do? One word, people: *Pez!* You walk up, pull out your Pez dispenser, and you say,

"Pez?"

The offer will bring about one of three reactions:

1. The girl laughs because she thinks the Pez routine is a cute and comical way of introducing yourself. You know from this reaction that she has a decent sense of humor (or at least that she's amused by you). Dude, you're in.

2. She's confused by the Pez routine at first, but you can tell that her confusion turns to interest in either you or your technique. Dude, you're in.

3. She looks at you like you're the biggest dork on the face of the planet. Fine, so you're not in, but look at it this way: Who the hell would want to be with a girl who's that stuck-up? Not me. If she doesn't have a sense of humor and can't appreciate the Pez approach, personally, I don't even want to know her, let alone spend any extended period of time with her.

Okay, so let's say you got reaction one or two. You've started a conversation. It was that simple.

You can now ask her whatever you want. "What's your name?" "Where do you go to school?" "Are you here with friends?" "Would you like to get naked on my parents' kitchen counter anytime soon?"

Dude, you're *so* in.

Now hopefully, many of you are wondering what kind of Pez dispenser you should purchase. These types of questions are important to ask, because women notice detail. Your Pez character will determine how girls will perceive you. After all, it *is* a first impression. I own many different characters so I can choose who I'm going to roll with based on my mood and the occasion.

Sometimes I'll go with Wonder Woman, when I want to let a girl know I'm down with a strong-willed, kick-ass female. Or I might go with Bugs Bunny, because he's got style. Daisy Duck is a good call when you want to

Ladies,
I would advise you to *not* accept a small sugary tablet from any guy at a bar or a club.

show you have a sensitive side. Garfield is solid because he's such a smart-ass. It's your choice. Pick the Pez dispenser that suits you.

The Second "In"

Funny-face.

You're at a party or a dance and you see a girl you want to talk to. Your eyes meet across the dance floor—and you both look away. You don't know if this means anything, because initial eye contact can be accidental. Then, there it is! *Second* eye contact! This means either she's interested or for some freak reason you made accidental eye contact twice. You try to act cool, but deep down you know you look like a total dork.

There is a way to remedy this situation. The *next* time you make secondary eye contact, smile briefly, then put your thumb on your nose, wiggle the other four fingers on your hand, and make a funny face:

Funny-face is similar to the Pez technique. If the girl laughs because she thinks you're funny or that your

AN IMPORTANT WARNING: You want to make sure to smile playfully while you're making the funny face so that it is clear you're not trying to make fun of the girl you want to impress. A misinterpreted funny face can end in hurt feelings or, worse, physical pain when she slaps you across your face. Be sure your expression is positive and playful and leaves nothing up for interpretation.

technique is adorable, then you walk over and introduce yourself.

You're in.

If she looks at her friend with an "Oh my God, who is this loser?" expression, then you've just encountered a woman with a very large stick up her ass. Again, no one in their right mind should want to be with a girl like that—no matter how hot she may be. She has a bad attitude and no sense of humor. You've just done yourself a favor by eliminating the possibility of having to go on a date with this girl. The funny-face technique creates a win-win situation.

The Third "In"

Call me crazy, but here's one final idea: You see a girl you like. You walk up to her and say, "Hi, my name's Colin." (Although if your name isn't Colin, I wouldn't use 'Colin'.) "I noticed you from across the way and I wanted to come meet you."

It's standard, but effective. This may in fact be the best way to meet a girl. It's easy, and she won't think you're trying too hard. However, it's blatantly honest and takes balls to pull off. If she shoots you down, there's nothing to hide behind. You're either in or you're shot down like an unlucky bird migrating south for the winter.

Personally, I'll stick with Pez or funny-face. But that's just me. I think those ins go well with my personality. Try them out. See if they work for you. If not, come up with something that suits *your* personality. I want to stress that attracting women isn't about adopting my techniques. On the contrary, attracting women is about using an in that works and is comfortable for you. Be yourself. Be confident, and you can't lose.

"Situational ins"

Okay, so now you know how to create "general ins" but how do you create "situational ins"? Meaning, how do you put yourself in the right place at the right time to meet the girl of your dreams?

First, you need to get involved in as many activities as possible. The more groups you associate with, the better chance you have of meeting people (people = *women*).

So let's say you're single. When you list the qualities of your ideal girlfriend, you place "into emo" and "would consider talking to me if we were trapped together in a two-person tent during a rainstorm" at the top of the list. But how will you ever meet a girl like that? I'll tell you how.

Chicks who dig emo are sensitive ladies—the kinds of girls who are members of the drama club, or who study art. So get up off the couch and register for photography class. Try out for a part in the school play. If you don't want to act, then become a part of the stage crew. Also, visit the gym and check out the female athletes.

Place yourself around girls who share your interests. Pretty soon, they'll begin to recognize you and want to know more about who you are. You'll be getting closer to them in no time.

But what about those situations that just fall into your lap? Those moments when it seems as if God himself (herself?) is smiling down on you. How do you take advantage of them? I'll give you an example: You walk into your Spanish class a couple of minutes before the bell is going to ring. You spot a girl you're interested in. She's seated. There is an open seat next to her. What do you do? You freak out and run to the little boy's room, right? Wrong. You *sit next to her*.

Just like that, you've created your situational in.

Once you've managed to secure a seat beside her, your next move is to get her number. Ask if she'll exchange phone numbers in case either of you are absent and need to find out the homework assignment. You do this to give the initial impression that you're *a little bit* interested in her. However, if you ask her without asking anybody else, she might think you're *too* into her. She'll get suspicious.

Therefore, you want to ask the person next to her as well, so that she thinks it's a legitimate request. After you ask the person next to this girl, ask her for her number as a backup plan (in case you can't get in touch with your other classmate).

Do you run the risk of sounding like a dork if you act like you're super-eager to stay on top of schoolwork? Sure. *However, you can always counter sounding like a dork by acting uninterested in what you're doing.* Start by phrasing sentences like this:

"Yeah, I was wondering if it's cool if I get your number, too. Just in case something comes up with class or whatever?"

You see how when you say it like this you sound aloof and cool?

On the contrary, if you were to say it like the guy in my next example, you wouldn't have a chance in hell with this girl:

"Yes, I am curious to know if I can copy down your number as well, in case Veronica is sick and I desperately need to get the assignment."

Saying something like that will ruin you before you even have a shot. If you find yourself sounding like the human boner above, then change the way you word things. Phraseology can make a great deal of difference with women.

This is what we call "being the cool guy." Girls love Cool Guy.

. . .

Let's recap. You start with creating general ins, like Pez and funny-face, that you can use in any situation. Then you learn how to create situational ins to put yourself in the right place at the right time. Like sitting next to a girl in class. You then act *a little bit* interested in her (this may simply be done by exchanging phone numbers), and revert to playing it cool (acting unaffected by her presence).

It sounds stupid, but it works.

The Many Faces of the Ladies' Man

Cool Guy

So you've made contact with a girl. You've exchanged phone numbers. Now what?

You have to be smart about how you deal with girls away from school. Act too interested, and you'll turn them off. Act completely uninterested, and she'll think you're a jerk. You need to strike a delicate balance between the two if you want to get this relationship going.

For example, let's say Spanish-class girl calls you at home for the homework assignment because she was absent from school. You don't want to tell her what the assignment is right away.

You have to be Cool Guy.

So she calls, the ring vibrates your drum, and you pick up:

"Hey, it's Kelly. I was just wondering if you could give me the assignment because I wasn't feeling well today and didn't make it to school."

Your initial impulse is to give her the assignment immediately.

That is not cool.

Listen up: *We (guys) have to fight many of our initial impulses with women.*

Impulses. You know when you have to take a crap at an amusement park so bad that it starts to crown? If we followed our impulses, we'd crap our pants on the spot. But we don't. Why? Because unless we want to smell like shit for the rest of the day, we have to fight that initial impulse and wait for the comfort, cleanliness, and privacy of a toilet seat and some toilet paper.

Now apply the crowning theory to Kelly.

You should take your time, enjoy the moment, and get to know her.

Don't shit your pants!

She can't hang up until you give her the homework assignment. So why don't you sit back, relax, and chat with her a bit? You can bring up other topics to get to know her as a person and not just as a study-buddy or a classmate. This will also give her a chance to get to know you.

So what's your next move?

What would Cool Guy do?

Well, she said she's sick. Cool Guy would ask her what's wrong.

This will provide conversation that isn't based on school. She'll tell you, and then you'll say:

"Oh, man. That sucks, I hope you're starting to feel better."

You hear yourself say this, and you realize that Cool Guy is taking over. You continue:

"Let me go grab the assignment. I think it's in my bag."

The assignment is sitting right next to you. You were working on it when the phone rang, but you're not going to give her the impression that you were planted there doing your homework.

Cool Guy has officially taken over.

You'll act like you were watching a basketball game, or rehearsing your lines for the play, or practicing your song for chorus. Anything but homework. See, deep down, women want someone who is smart and dedicated when it comes to school, but they certainly don't want to think you're a nerd. They want to know that you do well in school but that you don't obsess about it. Cool Guy gets all A's but never brags. He doesn't care about school when he's not there.

It's about being *relaxed.*

Remember, it sounds stupid, but it works. You have to act like Cool Guy to get a girl interested.

So you're going to give her the assignment, but before you hang up, make another connection between the two of you that isn't about school. Ask her,

"So who's there taking care of you?"

This way you'll not only sound concerned, you'll find out about her personal life. Are her parents together? Are they divorced? What type of relationship does she have with them? Does she wear a thong or granny panties? Maybe the two of you have something in common (hopefully not the granny panties). Treat her like you would treat anyone else you wanted to get to know. In other words, *talk to her.*

So far, you're playing this perfectly. You're being cool, sensitive, and slightly aloof, all at the same time. This is the balance you want to achieve. You asked her if she was okay and at the same time you acted chill about the homework assignment. Here is where you make the only *totally* nice-guy move of the conversation.

"Hey, since you're not feeling well, why don't I work on the assignment for a little while and come over and just let you look at mine?"

How perfect is that? She may say that she doesn't want your help. However, even if she says no, she'll still think you're a sweetheart for offering.

Bonus points.

If she says yes, then you get to go to her house, see her outside of school, and begin to develop a relationship with her.

The reason I say that this is the only *totally* nice-guy move is because you never want to be *overly* nice to girls (if you want to keep them interested). Girls want a challenge. They don't want someone who would clearly give his left nut just to sit next to them.

This is a concept that escaped my friends and me in high school, and we suffered the consequences: very few ladies.

We couldn't understand why the assholes always got the girls.

When I say "girls," I mean younger girls. When women reach their mid-twenties or forties or fifties, depending on how they mature, they begin to choose guys differently. That's when being the *full-time* nice guy pays off.

But when women are younger, you have to act sort of indifferent to get them to like you. Once you have them, you can show them what it's like to be with a nice guy.

Ladies,

Why can't you make it easier on us by once, just once, deciding to choose the nice guy instead of the difficult guy? Why must you select and tolerate the assholes? Try the guy who is going to treat you well for a change.

When they've had a taste of that, they won't go back to dating losers again.

I know, it's very complicated. We'll talk about how to treat women if you become a couple later. Right now all you need to know is how to *attract* them.

So repeat after me:

I WILL ACT INDIFFERENT.

I WILL ACT ALOOF.

I WILL BE COOL GUY.

. . .

One point I want to stress is that we shouldn't *actually* be indifferent, aloof, or assholes as guys. Deep down we have to be attentive, caring, and loving people. Nice guys. The only problem is that if we acted how we felt and played the *super-nice* card, girls would lose interest very fast. And it's not a gender thing. Guys are the same way. *People want what they can't have.* They want the chase. Girls want to chase you. Even Tupac understood what I'm saying (may he rest in peace):

"Girl you gotta tease me, I don't want it if it's that easy. . . ."

I need to point this out because I'm not encouraging guys to disrespect women. I'm creating a practical vehicle to get you close to girls. Once you are dating her, you can be as open, honest, caring, and loving as you truly are.

A Ladies' Man doesn't enjoy deceiving women. He realizes that he has to learn some basics to interacting with women in order to allow relationships to blossom.

. . .

Let's recap. Create general ins. Create situational ins. Act a little bit interested. Revert to Cool Guy. Being Cool Guy includes acting somewhat indifferent and aloof. However, you are just acting. Deep down you are a sweet guy who desires to get to a point where you can show your woman a heart full of love and honesty.

Confident Guy

Women are attracted to confidence. Confidence makes women trust you, makes them desire you, and makes them want to spend time with you.

Up to bat: Confident Guy.

Confident Guy has a general level of security in any situation. Confident Guy enters the room with a sense of "I don't care what you think of me, because I'm just here to have a good time." Women pick up on positive, strong energy. No matter what situation you encounter, feeling free about who you are and what you do has an unmistakable effect on both you and the women around you. Confident Guy just wants to chill out and enjoy himself.

Sometimes Confident Guy walks into a room with his pants down just for shits and giggles. With a confident attitude you'll be fine with the ladies, no matter what happens. Just the other day I was playing pool with a couple of my friends. We ended up playing doubles against these two hot girls we didn't know. One of the girls pointed out to me and everyone else in the room that my fly was down.

I stayed confident: "Yeah, I know. It's hot down there. I don't want him to overheat."

I left my crotch unzipped.

No matter what happens, you gotta trust that you're the man.

If we never said, "I don't know if she likes me," or "I don't think I can ask her out," do you realize how many more women we would meet and date? Confident Guy doesn't doubt himself. He doesn't think, "I can't ask *her* out." And even if he does, he doesn't let it stop him. He goes up and asks the girl out anyway.

Even Mark Twain was a Ladies' Man back in his day. He said:

"Courage is not the lack of fear, but acting in spite of it."

It takes balls of steel to know your apprehensions and stroll right through them.

Social Guy

We all know a super-social guy, and to some extent we all envy him. He's the guy who plays two sports, is in the choir, is the lead in the school play, takes all honors classes, and makes time on the side to volunteer for the Special Olympics and scoop up after the neighbor's dog.

Social Guy is friends with the jocks, the freaks, the geeks, and everyone in between. Why? Because *he's* all of those things himself. He doesn't let one thing define him. He is everything. He belongs to all kinds of clubs and teams. Basketball function? He's there. Debate team? He's the captain. Advanced Placement study session for Spanish? Bingo! (Social Guy speaks fluent Spanish.) And when the choirgirl, drama girl, and cheerleader girl feel like having an orgy . . . Social Guy is going to be there with bells on and a leopard G-string.

Besides the orgies, it's just more fun to be Social Guy.

His name gets mentioned everywhere. Student government is organizing a rally and they need someone to get a group of volunteers together—Social Guy can do that. A cute girl needs a study-buddy—Social Guy to the rescue. Invitations to a huge party need to be handed out. They're probably going to contact Social Guy.

I don't know how much clearer I can make this. You have no choice. If you desire to meet more women, then get out and be social. Put the controller to your Xbox down and get out of the house . . . now!

Speaking of invitations to parties . . .

Party Guy

Attending parties can make you an immediate member of the social scene. Instead of asking you:

"Do you know when the next test is?"

The ladies will be asking you,

"Are you going to that huge party tonight?"

Why will they ask you this? Because they will have seen you at parties before and they'll know you're part of that scene.

I can already hear your response: "But I don't get invited to the parties." Take a tissue, wipe those tears away, and listen up. I have two words for you: CRASH THEM! That's how I started my friendships with three of my best friends (and how we all started to meet the ladies).

We, like many, didn't get invited to the parties and spent most of our high-school lives powdering our balls at home on Friday nights.

Well, one night I was hanging out with my friend Casey when Mike and Trevor, two guys we had never really hung out with, called. The conversation went something like this:

Trevor: "Colin, we found out where this one party is."

Colin: "Are we invited?"

Trevor: "No."

Mike (in the background): "Course not."

Colin: "Cool, pick Casey and me up in an hour."

And just like that we were on the map as far as the high-school social scene went. Sure it's weird (aka scary as hell) walking up to a party when you're not invited. At that first party with Trevor, Casey, and Mike, one of the football jocks actually looked us over as we entered and said, "What are *you* guys doing here?" He wasn't trying to be a dick (I think it came naturally). The comment was genuine; he couldn't understand why we were there.

There were countless times when we were denied entrance to parties when—and don't worry, this *will* happen to you—there was a list and we weren't on it.

You may think you'd rather sit on one of your balls than feel rejection like that and, well, you'd be right. But the risk of getting denied or humiliated by a football player (or any other piece of fecal matter who isn't nice to "uncool kids") is well worth taking when you manage to get in and party your balls off. Remember that there's security and strength in numbers. Go to these parties with friends, and if it doesn't work out, then bail and go somewhere else. If it does work out, enjoy yourself.

When you get into the party, do yourself a favor and don't stand in a circle with the same four guys you came with. In my experience, that's pretty much what most parties end up being: everybody standing in a circle with the people they arrived with. If you think about it, you could save yourself the time and energy by buying a keg, blasting your stereo at home, and talking to your friends in the middle of your living room at the top of your lungs.

Be the Party Guy. Don't guard the keg or stand in a corner. Go talk to people. Talk to *women*. Don't try to talk to certain people just because you think they're "popular." Keep it real.

While I understand the pressures and the bullshit associated with the social scene, there's nothing worse than a tool who will do anything in his power to be "popular." Those people are known as ass-kissers, and they end up becoming very unpopular later in life.

Talk to people who interest you, the ones you think are genuinely cool. They're probably the people like you who don't feel totally comfortable at parties, either.

Partying, meeting girls, and spending social time with your friends are all very important parts of being a guy. When I look back, I remember the crazy parties, the drama, the hookups, the girls, and all the people I cared about. If you channel Party Guy, that's what *you'll* remember, too. Not your grade on the midterm or how many *Star Trek* episodes you could watch in a row on a Friday night. You'll remember times well spent with friends and ladies (I must point out that members of my immediate and extended family are "Trekkies," and I mean no disrespect to their kind).

Keep in mind that you don't have to join somebody else's social scene if you don't want to. Create one of your own, instead. Make your own lists. Throw your own parties. Start hanging out with people you enjoy spending time with.

Having a life doesn't have to be synonymous with standing in someone's backyard at 12:00 A.M. waiting for the cops to break up the party. You can go to museums, coffee shops, or whatever makes you happy. Do what *you* want to do. Just get out there and *do* it.

Mike Murray

My friend Mike doesn't know much, but he knows one thing: Girls love it when guys can dance. Not just when guys *can* dance but even when guys *try* to dance. Guys attract women by getting out on the dance floor and having a good time without caring what they look like.

So be like Mike. Whenever you can, go and get your groove on.

Don't be afraid to turn the music on at home and practice your moves. I'm sure if you ask people, they will deny that they practice their dance moves at home in front of the mirror, but we all know it goes on. I dance around the house by myself for fun (and for practice) all the time. Usually naked, but that's a whole other story altogether.

You *have* to dance.

So much can happen when dancing that can't happen in any other situation. Dancing creates a specific sexual vibe. Where else can you see a girl you know and within minutes end up grinding against her? Nowhere. That's the beauty of dancing. Besides the fact that it's sexy and girls love guys who dance, it's just plain fun to shake that ass every now and then. Dancing is a good release of energy.

I can't tell you how many times (well, I probably could, but I won't) my friends and I met girls while we were out dancing. I think it's rare for women to see a group of guys who like to dance. When they do find guys like me and my friends dancing, they know they can go out on the dance floor and have a good time with us.

Bueno Para Bailar

So you're out dancing and a girl catches your eye. You move over to her and start dancing next to her. You'll either get an inviting vibe or an uninviting vibe.

This is paramount.

For a girl, there's nothing more annoying than having a guy follow her around all night long when she's not interested. (Do you want some sweaty, horny girl, whom you don't find attractive, following you around all night trying to attach herself to you?)

You have to take the hint. If you don't take the hint, you look pathetic. If you look pathetic, you lose your membership to the Ladies' Man Club.

If you get denied, have the confidence to think, "All right, she didn't want me, but the next person will."

Do not stalk these girls! Look for somebody else who intrigues you and move on.

A good sign that she's not interested is if she turns her back to you when you're approaching.

However, I must point out that there are those occasions when a girl gives you the backside as an invitation. She might be looking for a little backside grinding.

Gentlemen, you have to be careful about approaching the ass. Freaking an uninterested booty is grounds for expulsion from the Ladies' Man Club. That's why you need to feel the situation out (figuratively). Start dancing behind her. You'll be able to find out pretty quickly if her body is into it. If the body language isn't there, back away and see what happens. If she moves back into you and keeps shakin' it, then you know she wants you to continue. If she's trying to get the heck away from you as quick as possible—she isn't interested.

Either that or she felt your boner.

This is why my preferred method is to approach face-to-face. This way you can see the interest in a girl's eyes. And once you catch that spark, you can jump on it.

Don't hesitate on the dance floor. Hesitation shows a lack of confidence. You have to believe that you're the man—and make girls believe it, too. Approach the girl and start dancing with her.

Don't go straight to freaking her (aka grinding, up close and personal). That's the sign of a desperate, horny bastard.

First, get a little distance in between the two of you and check the scenario. See if she wants you to move closer to her. If you see the sparks in her eyes turn to flames that can't be fanned, get the midsection ready to begin grinding.

Freak, Freak, Y'all

When you freak a girl, just go with the rhythm. Usually a standard movement will be established by one of you, and you just keep repeating that motion (switching it up to the music when necessary). Stay attentive to her body language. Do *not* lose your cool and do something stupid like grab her ass. At this point, within reason, you can do no wrong.

Well, besides getting the dreaded . . .

Dance-Floor Boner

It happens to the best of us.

The key is not *how to avoid* getting hard-ons while you're dancing with girls, but *what to do* once you get the boner. Because let's face it, the woody is inevitable. How could it not be? You're standing there, rubbing your penis up against her vulva, with a couple centimeters of clothing separating the two erogenous zones.

We have no choice. The penis has a mind of its own.

Now, there are two schools of thought when it comes to the boner on the dance floor. I will give you both and let you decide which you prefer:

Ladies,
    If a guy is stalking you on the dance floor, just turn around and say, "I have a boyfriend, and I'd like it if you left me alone." You don't have to be nice to some freak who won't take a hint.

1.) Letting her have it

I have friends who swear by this technique. They figure that since you're freaking each other, you both know you're getting turned on (probably you more than her), so you continue to dance and let the girl feel your boner. After all, it's natural, and some guys want to let a girl know how turned on they are.

So they lay the wood down.

I find this dangerous, because although there will be some girls who don't mind (and may even like) the idea that they're turning you on, I have a pretty strong suspicion that most girls don't want to be jabbed with a stiffy.

2.) The tuck-under method

Please refer to page 39 for information on how to execute the TUM.

The Rules of Attraction

I am including two final sections that I think are important for you to consider before we close out part one. These sections can help you get around stumbling blocks (that every guy encounters) so that you don't accidentally throw back the biggest fish in the pond.

1.) Perfection

Most guys are constantly measuring girls up to a benchmark that doesn't exist: perfection. The right girl has to have The Perfect Body. The Perfect Face. The Perfect Personality.

The reality is that *there is no perfection.* I know this may be hard for some of you to believe, but not even *I* am perfect. Now I know you (like millions of people all around the world) are thinking, "But Colin, of course you are flawless in every way, shape, and form!" Fair enough. But while I may seem like a model of perfection, like the ideal man, like a god of sorts, even I get an occasional zit. (If you need a break from reading because of the unbelievable preceding information, then you are not alone.) Here's the real deal: *All* healthy female bodies are beautiful. Unique faces that distinguish us from one another are attractive. The perfect personality is one that meshes nicely with yours.

"Perfection" is an ideal that we're forced to consume by big business and the media. Nothing, in the real world (yeah, I know) is perfect. Our flaws are what make us human, they're what make us unique, and if we could put our models of perfection aside and just concentrate on the real women in our lives, I think we would be much happier.

2.) Chemistry

When you're looking for a girl to date, you shouldn't just try to conquer a woman that everyone else thinks is "hot"; you should pursue the girl you feel a chemical bond with.

Why?

Because you shouldn't be looking for a certain type of girl just to please someone else. For instance, have you ever noticed that many female models look like space aliens? I don't want to date a Martian just because Dave Howard from Little Rock, Arkansas, masturbated to her picture in the latest Victoria's Secret catalogue.

I agree that looks are important. They're what draw you to someone in the first place. They're just not the deciding factors I use when I choose who I will pursue.

I recently dated a girl whom I would never have dated two years ago. She's not what people consider "hot." But there was something about her . . . something I couldn't explain. I thought I would give it a chance—and it turned out that we clicked. She was smart, pretty (though not traditionally speaking), and an all-around cool chick.

It was not my admiration of her looks that fueled my desire to be with her; it was "chemistry." The chemistry that grew from talking, sharing, and spending time with each other. From learning to appreciate each other on a deep, personal level. When I looked at her I wanted to kiss her. Hug her. Hold her. *That's* chemistry.

For me, chemistry is more important than looking for whatever type of woman my friends, society, or my family tells me is "good looking."

Chemistry is a feeling you get in your gut about a girl.

Don't let an amazing girl slip away just because she doesn't meet society's standards of beauty. She could be a dynamite person whom you'll have great chemistry with. I've passed over a lot of girls because I was too concerned with what somebody else thought was "pretty." I don't want you to make the same mistake.

We've covered the basics of what a guy needs to know about his body and about attracting a woman's attention.

This means that *you* now know how to get a girl to notice you and how to grease your gumballs. I know many guys who can get this far but can't go the distance. To be a Ladies' Man, you not only have to catch a girl's eye, you have to know how to act and when to act when she shows interest.

The first chapter in this section deals with dating. You will learn when to call after getting her phone number and how to succeed during the sweat-inducing first call. I'll also suggest how to best escape becoming the "friend" of a girl you want to date (girls always try to make the nice guy their friend). Because we don't want to be their friends, do we? No. We want to be their boyfriends, or at least the guy lying in bed next to them at night.

I will teach you how to ask a girl out and how to know whether you are "going on a date" or "just hanging out."

In one of my prouder moments, I will divulge how you can impress, entertain, and even spark a party in your pants by treating a woman to free frozen food. You will discover good places to take your dates, and we'll delve into one of the scariest moments of the dating game: walking her to her door and attempting a good-night kiss (we'll also discuss kissing techniques that will ensure a trip to second or third base).

The second chapter is entitled Seeing Girls. Here we will deliberate about seeing girls you *don't* want to eventually make your girlfriend, and seeing girls you *do* ultimately want to go out with. I'll show you the proper way of introducing the girls you are seeing, how to understand the games girls play, and finally, how to facilitate the transition from seeing a girl to being boyfriend and girlfriend.

The third chapter is about Girlfriends. We start this section on a bit of an awkward note when I tell you about the different pooches I've screwed (aka huge mistakes I've made). Then we'll shift gears to pinpoint the difference between jealous boyfriends, controlling boyfriends, and cool boyfriends. Then we tackle how to give and receive proper "space" in a relationship (so that you have time to do you own thing and hang out with your friends), and finally, we end on a lighter note: breaking up.

4
Dating

"You know that look women get when they want sex?
Me neither."
—STEVE MARTIN

I've created a universal system to define the states of relationships. There are three stages.

1.) "Dating" women

2.) "Seeing" women

3.) "Going out" with women

Dating is when you ask a girl out and go out with her

for the first few dates. At this point you're just getting to know each other to see if there's any interest.

Seeing a girl is when you're past the first few dates and you are spending time with a girl on a regular basis. Either one of you may "see" or "date" other people at this stage.

Going out is when the two of you have decided that you are boyfriend and girlfriend. Neither one of you is going to "see" or "date" anyone else, unless you decide to break up.

Got it?

Good.

So you took care of your style, got her attention with an in, channeled Cool Guy, and stayed confident. You have her phone number, and you can tell that she's into you. It's time to call her.

When to Call After Getting Her Number

This is a long-debated question among guys. Some only wait a day, some wait a week, and some never call at all. I think the sooner you do it, the better chance you have of being fresh in her mind. If you call earlier rather than later, she'll remember when she gave you her phone number, instead of thinking you're some freak who just bummed her number off of one of her friends.

So how long should you wait to call? I say between one and three days. That's your best bet in my book (and this *is* my book).

The First Call

The first call is a difficult task. You pick up the phone about six hundred times and dial all but one of her

SIDE NOTE: *Don't ever solicit a girl's number from somebody other than her.* This approach is offensive and negates your chances of creating interest. Why? Because you haven't given her the option of saying no when you ask if you can call her. It's an intrusion into her space, and you may come off looking like a stalker. If *she* gives you her number, she has agreed to let you call her. And that's better for everyone involved.

numbers. Then you sit there on the last number, scared shitless to press it.

If you punch it in, there's no turning back, in the day and age of *69 and Caller ID. If a girl finds out that you've been calling and hanging up on her, you just threw away your one and only chance.

Now she thinks you're a stalker.

Or a coward.

I remember first calls. Heart pounding. Shallow breathing. Adrenaline pumping through my body like never before. I press the last digit of her phone number on my fourteenth attempt and just sit there waiting for God to intervene.

The phone starts to ring.

Oh my God, what do I say if her mom picks up?

Or what if it's her dad and he thinks I'm some kind of pervert?

What if she doesn't remember me?

Holy shit, I think this is a bad idea.

She picks up. "Hello," she says in her sweet voice.

I can't breathe.

"Hey, this is Colin from English class."

Phone Fear

Dead air on the phone is a total killer. I lived in fear of silent pauses whenever I called a girl. So to avoid them while you're still relatively inexperienced, do what I did. Keep a little pad of paper next to the phone with ideas of things that you think would be "cool" to talk about. Movies, TV shows, or other people at school are all good topics of conversation. Use the paper in case of an emergency.

I feel like the biggest nerd on the face of the planet.

"Oh, hey, what's going on?"

And from there it's all up to you. You got your in and called her on the phone. Now talk to her. Get to know her. You're the man if you get this far. The victory has been won, because you've given yourself a chance. Even if you crash and burn, you're still a hero. Now you just have to be intuitive and see if she's interested in you.

Trust me, you'll be able to tell if she's titillated by the way she talks to you. Whether she's trying to give off the "friend" vibe, or the "I wouldn't mind shoving my tongue in your mouth" vibe.

When to Ask Her Out

Don't have more than two conversations on the phone without making plans to do something. You should ask her on a date by the second or third time you talk to her.

If you don't show interest in going out on dates with her, then you are, without question, going to become the "friend."

Who else would talk to a girl on the phone endlessly without asking her out on a date? Nobody but a friend. Or a gay guy.

Ten words: No, no, no, no, no. Do not let this happen.

Let her know early on that you like her romantically. Force her to shoot you down if she doesn't like you in that way. Don't leave it so that you'll always be wondering if she likes you as more than a friend. It's better to try, and have her rip your freakin' heart out with her bare hands, than to not try. Remember, it was old-school Ladies' Man Alfred Lord Tennyson who said, *"'Tis better to have loved and lost than never to have loved at all."*

Alfred knew what was up.

• • •

During your initial phone calls you can talk about school if it's something the two of you have in common. However, you are forbidden from letting the academic part of school dominate the conversation. If you talk about school, talk about something other than classes. Talk about mutual friends or parties that you've heard about and plan on going to. Talk about TV shows, movies, music, or cool books that you've read (like this one). Talk about anything but what grade you got on the most recent test.

Remember: Cool Guy doesn't care about school when he's not there.

What you care about is going out with this girl. So let her know who you are. Talk about your interests, what you're passionate about, where you're from, what your family is like; do everything you can to get to know her as a human being and not just as a classmate.

Pretty soon, she'll start to feel a bond with you. And if you ask her out promptly, that bond will be more than the friend bond.

It'll be the "let's get it on" bond.

How to Ask Her Out

It's simple.

I didn't say "easy." I said "simple." And the uncomplicated things in life are often the hardest to see your way through.

During the second conversation, you have to "nut up" and ask her out. (*Nut up* is a poetic phrase my high-school basketball coach used when he thought we were playing like "wussies." Half wimp, half pussy.)

Now, you have to be careful about *how* you ask her out, because the way you phrase it will determine whether she thinks you're "hanging out" (as friends) or going out on a "date."

It is very important to make this distinction as soon as possible. If you're going to go through the heart-pounding, sweaty palms, blackouts, and all the other crap you'll experience before saying the actual words, you might as well make sure it's a *date*.

Before I give you practical examples of the different ways to ask a girl out, let's talk a little about how and why to avoid becoming the "friend."

Limbo Land

There's a dangerous area in any blossoming relationship where both the guy and the girl don't know if they're going to be friends, or lovers. When I say "lovers" I don't mean you have to be doing the wild-

Ladies,

Can you do us (guys) a favor and just tell us straight up if there's no chance of us getting past the "friend" status? It would make our lives so much easier. Don't worry about "hurting our feelings" or "being a bad person" or "not showering daily"; it's okay to not like us. It's just not okay to let us persevere on the issue for months. Keep in mind that a guy has to be hit over the head with the fact that you don't like him romantically, or he will keep trying to hump you like an ape in heat.

monkey dance, I just mean having a romantic relationship instead of a platonic one (*platonic relationship:* a relationship that doesn't *in any way* involve your penis and her vagina). Granted, there are some girls that you solely want to be friends with. That's great. Platonic friendships with women will be some of the most rewarding relationships you have in your life (as they have been for me), but right now we're not talking about friends. We're talking about the hotties that you want to swim around with—naked—in a giant pool filled with Jell-O.

It's important to stay away from the area I call *limbo land* with girls that you want to date. In limbo land you drift around aimlessly as the friend, and all chances of becoming the romantic love interest dissipate.

In my experience, once you're the friend, there's no going back. You'll be the friend with that girl for the rest of your relationship.

And each time you hang out with this girl you'll be reminded (by your heart, your mind, and your penis) that you still want her. You will continually feel rejected when she doesn't reciprocate the feelings that you have for her.

In other words, constantly hanging out with a girl you like who has banished you to limbo land is like accidentally cutting your thumb open while slicing a carrot, then deciding that in the future you are going to slash your thumb *every* time you prepare dinner.

You have to give yourself every shot at becoming the love interest of the girl you want, because limbo land can be an ugly, thumbless place to be.

Avoiding the "Friend" Trap

If the girl that you like has a boyfriend, the first thing you should do is avoid talking about him, and the same goes for any guy she is dating, or any guy she wants to date.

This is difficult, because if a girl wants to talk about the men in her life, our first inclination is to indulge her desire.

But remember how we have to fight many of our initial impulses with women? Our initial impulse here is to talk about her relationship problems. We think it'll be a great way to get to know her. And maybe, if we can get her to think about these problems, she'll leave the guy she's dating!

Don't shit your pants. It doesn't work that way.

Would Cool Guy talk to this girl about a guy she is dating?

No.

The reality of this situation is that when you start talking about a guy she's dating, you're automatically lumped into the category of "sensitive guy friend" because you are listening to her, and not coming on to her.

Get a grip.

Later in life you'll learn that it is possible to be the sensitive guy friend *and* the love interest, because women wise up and learn that they want the nice guys. Like I said, this happens somewhere between the ages of twenty and a hundred. Men wise up—somewhere between the ages of ninety-eight and a hundred—and realize that it's not all about a tight body. (By the way, the average male life span in the United States is seventy-two.)

Women get past the years of seeking out what's bad for them, and they end up wanting a guy who can be a friend *and* a lover.

But what do you do in the meantime?

Avoid talking to her about other guys, period.

In fact, as soon as you hear her tell you she's interested in another guy, change the subject. For example:

"I think Dave is really hot."

Your response has to be quick, yet calculated.

"Hey, we should go out this weekend."

Nice work. Not only have you avoided the Dave comment, but you've also taken initiative to express your interest in her and show her that you're confident. You heard her say she thinks Dave's hot, and you still had the balls to ask her out.

Of course, you have to realize that she was probably trying to accomplish one of three things with the "Dave" comment:

1. She was either telling you she thinks he's hot in order to send the message that she is *not* interested in you as a boyfriend.

2. She said it to play hard to get (Cool Girl).

3. She said it to try and gauge how you feel about her. (This may seem strange to you, but such is the female.)

By asking her out quickly, you eliminate the bullshit of playing games. You don't have to think about why she made the comment about Dave, because you don't care what she thinks about Dave. You care about whether she wants to go out with *you*.

You're learning, my friend.

A "Date" vs. "Hanging Out"

Okay, so now you know how and why to avoid becoming the friend. When you work up the nerve to ask her out—WHICH YOU WILL—you need to word the question (or non-question) with precision and be attentive to her response. I'll give you a couple of mock conversations, and you tell me how you think it's going.

Response #1

Colin: "We should go out sometime."

Girl: "Yeah, we should get a big group of people together. . . . You know, some of your friends and some of mine. It'll be fun."

Notice how I worded the question like Cool Guy. I didn't say, "Would you like to go out sometime with me on an official date?" Instead, I asked her casually (like I only sort of cared about her response). I played it smooth.

How do you think the conversation went?

If you think that the probability that she likes you is low, then you're using what little brain we men have. Her answer is leaning toward "hanging out," and you don't want to go there. Look out for phrases like "big group of people," or "Yeah, we should *all* do something." It means that she probably doesn't see you two being involved in a relationship.

However, there are a couple of additional possibilities. She may want to be around friends in order to feel more comfortable on a first date. Or maybe there's a party that she wants to go to with you *and* her friends.

You have to play this one out to see where it goes. If she *always* wants to bring people along, it's not a good sign. You may be entering friend territory. This requires immediate action, such as . . .

Response #2

Colin: "We should definitely go do something this weekend, just the two of us."

Girl: "Oh, I can't do it this weekend. I have something to do with my family."

Colin: "Okay, next weekend's cool."

Girl: "Next weekend I have to do something with my family as well."

Keep an eye on my wording. I specified that we would be going out on a date by saying "just the two of us." But even though I worded it correctly, good old Colin Mortensen has been shot down. He has lost his left wing, caught fire, and is torpedoing toward an immediate Earth-bound death.

The first time she said she had something to do with her family, it could have been a coincidence. After the second denial you have to take the hint. It is very possible that this girl may not like you. You *cannot* ask her out again; it's up to her now.

Therefore, you should end the conversation.

Colin: "Okay. No big deal. Have fun this weekend."

By doing this you put it in her hands. In the unlikely event that she really has to do something with her family both weekends, she'll call you and say that the following weekend is good for your date. If she doesn't say anything, then you know she wasn't interested.

Response #3

Colin: "Let's do something this weekend."

Girl: "Ummm, why don't you call me later? I'm not sure whether or not I have plans. I'll have to check my schedule."

Let me break the news to you before you call her back: If she says this, she's blowing you off.

She doesn't have plans. This is just an excuse to give her time to make up an event that she has to attend. You're done.

How do I know? Put yourself in the girl's shoes. If a girl you were interested in asked you out, would you say, "Let me check my schedule," or "Yeah, that sounds great"? I would opt for the latter.

I wouldn't call this girl back at all, but I'm easily offended and unforgiving. *You* can call her *just in case.* There's always the freak chance that she seriously didn't know if she had plans. Besides, if you've already been denied, then there's nothing left to lose.

Response #4

Colin: "We should go out soon."

Girl: "Yeah, I guess, that would be fine."

If she starts using phrases like "I guess" and adjectives like *fine,* you should seriously question why you are even considering going out with this girl. She's treating your proposed date like it's a trip to the proctologist. You may end up on a date with this girl, but chances are, there won't be a second.

Response #5

Colin: "Let's go out."

Girl: "No!"

There's not a whole lot of interpretation to do here. Look at it this way: If a girl says she doesn't want to go out with you, it's her loss (advice from my dad, a revered Ladies' Man). She's the one who's missing out, not you. You gotta have the confidence.

Alexander Graham Bell once said, "When one door closes, another opens."

He was talking about the door to his pants. His zipper.

Come on, you know he was talking about women. A.G.B. (that's what he likes me to call him) was getting crazy action from the ladies because he had the balls to get denied and go back out there and try again.

Not to mention the fact that he invented that telephone thing or whatever. Come to think of it, A.G.B. probably invented the telephone to ask women out (now there's a *serious* Ladies' Man).

The Only Good Response

Colin: "Do you wanna go out this weekend?"
Girl: "Sure! That sounds great!"
There you have it, gentlemen. The moment you've been waiting for. This is definitely "date" territory.

It might take you six attempts with six different girls to get one of them to say yes, but you have to be willing to be rejected the other five times in order to get here. The trick is staying on the pony until the ride is over. Try and maintain your confidence through the rejection.

If you can do that, you'll succeed at securing dates.

Great Places for Dates

If you're smart, by now you've called her two or three times and at the latest you asked her out on the third call. We'll assume that she said yes because, after all, you're a budding Ladies' Man.

What should you do now? Check out dating tip number one:

The ability to be prepared *and* spontaneous makes for a fun date.

So, first things first: You need to make a general plan. Each date's plan will depend on the girl and how you feel about her. Do you feel comfortable maintaining conversation all night? If so, try to avoid the movies. Does she eat Asian cuisine? If not, you might want to skip the Noodle Planet. Ask yourself these kinds of questions *before* you knock on her door.

Date #1

The most imaginative and unexpected dates are the ones that I enjoy. For that reason, I think that Chuck E. Cheese's is a great option. Chuck E. Cheese's is a place where six-year-olds go to have their birthday parties (it's also where I went for my twenty-first birthday party): pizza, video games, screaming children, and a mouse dressed up in a cheesy costume. This place has got romance written all over it.

The Cheese is an arcade and a carnival all in one. If the girl you're with doesn't like Chuck E Cheese's, then she's probably not a keeper. In my opinion, only the truly cool chicks will appreciate dinner and games with Chuck E.

Date #2

Another great date is taking a girl to Costco (Costco is one of those stores where they sell everything in bulk— a place where you can buy enough toilet paper to wipe your ass for a decade). Costco and other stores of its nature have certain nights when they set up different tables so that you can sample their food (really bad frozen food). Take her there to try all of the sample foods they're giving out.

Just cruise around the store tasting pizza pockets while considering the possibility of eating the same cereal for twenty years straight.

If Costco isn't your thing, hit another chain store. I think that Toys 'Я' Us is a great choice. Go to Toys 'Я' Us and walk around the store playing with all of the toys that aren't in packages. If you're lucky, they'll have a section of bikes and those miniature four-wheeling vehicles. *Then* it's on. You each choose a car or jeep and chase each other around the store.

• • •

The dates I described above are just two examples of my psychological and emotional dysfunction—I mean, *creativity*. Do whatever *you* think would be creative and fun. You can even do something standard, like taking her out to eat and then to a movie afterward. Going to an amusement park. Visiting the county fair. Bowling. Just *show her a good time*. Also, ask if there's anything she'd really like to do. If it sounds good to you, then take her there.

What to Bring for Your Date

I think you should always come to the door with a gift. I wouldn't bring a rose; a rose is too much of a cliché. Maybe a sunflower or something original that seems bright and happy. But then again, you really can't go wrong with . . .

PEZ!

That's right, folks, the universally accepted gift. (You

held up your lighters and Pez has made its return to *A New Ladies' Man*.)

Just bring something.

Who Pays for the Date?

The inviter is obliged to pay for the evening. Bottom line: If you invited, then you pay. You are the host for the evening on your date. If she invited, then she pays.

However, if she invited and plans on paying, *you must still offer to pay*. It might sound sexist, but that is what most women want you to do anyway: offer. If she aggressively tells you that she wants to pay, then put your wallet back in your pocket.

To tell you the truth, I pay no matter who invited who. But that could be because I'm Latin; it's a whole different story for me.

Beware. If you invited her on a date and she offers to go *dutch* (pay for half of the evening), then she might be trying to establish friend status. Keep your eyes open.

One thing is for sure: You need to make sure you have enough money. If you run out of money and she finds out, it could be the beginning of the end.

Dating is like war.

Always be prepared for your worst day.

The Good-Night Kiss

Let's assume that you had a great date. You drop her off at her house. Don't let her walk to the door alone. Get off your ass and walk her there—for two reasons.

1. It's common courtesy to see your date to the door to make sure she gets home safely.

2. Your thoughtfulness will increase your chances of getting a good-night kiss (or at least a good-night hug).

Now that you're on your way to her door, you've begun the most nerve-racking part of the evening. I'm sure there are guys out there who don't get nervous about the first kiss of the night, but I'm not one of them. I get more nervous than a van full of illegals headed for an armed border.

I know that there are a lot of circumstances in which you'll kiss her before the night is over—like if you're at a party and you see your opportunity (keep in mind that whenever you get your opportunity you must seize it immediately), but for now we'll assume that you haven't kissed her.

So you get to the door and the awkwardness begins. Don't just stand there like a human dildo. That's like having dead space on the first phone conversation. You need to minimize the bumbling, so act before the conversation gets uneasy. Tell her you had a great time, hold your hands out, and go in for the hug.

Ladies,

Make this good-night kiss moment as easy as possible on the guy. Be a Man's Woman. If you want to kiss him, then let him know in a cute way. You could say, "So, are you gonna kiss me now or what? I've been waiting all night." If you don't want to kiss him, if there's no chance of that going down, then say, "I just want to let you know that I don't kiss guys on the first date . . . but I had a great time."

The hug doesn't have to be weird.

My advice is to continue to hold her after the hug by keeping your hands on her waist and by backing your upper body away from hers, creating enough space to comfortably look into her eyes. When you continue to hold her like this, it lets her know that you plan on going in for the kiss.

Remember: Hesitation cripples even the strongest man. You *have* no time to hesitate if you keep your hands on her waist. Back your upper body away, keep your hands on her waist, look into her eyes for a brief moment, and then go in for the kiss.

Worst-case scenario, you get denied. It happens to the best of us (even Mike Murray).

Just remember what that one old guy said: It's better to try and get denied than to never try at all (I've taken a few liberties).

Kissing

There are many kissing techniques but in my experience, if you follow a few simple rules, you're guaranteed to succeed. Rule number one: **Never lead with an open mouth**. Don't go in with your tongue hanging out, either. You might've seen the open-mouth-leading-with-the-tongue technique used in a movie or music video, but real people don't kiss like that.

Don't model your sex life after Ron Jeremy's.

Rule number two: Give her warning before you go French. I almost always use a small peck to initiate the kissing (a soft kiss that captures her lower or upper lip with both of your lips). Then and only then, after the peck, may you involve your tongue in the kiss.

I have a friend who uses the "brush-the-cheek" method instead of the peck. He lightly strokes the girl's cheek with the back of his hand before he goes in for the first kiss. I don't recommend this technique because it's a little cheesy. I'm not saying it won't work. It just seems forced. Planned. Like you saw it in a movie and you're trying it out in real life. And as far as movies are concerned, art doesn't imitate life very much concerning sex.

Just be natural.

Be yourself.

Kissing a Porn Star

There are four classic mistakes once you get this far:

1.) Using too much tongue.

2.) Using too little tongue.

3.) Using lizard tongue.

4.) Keeping your eyes open.

Avoid these screwups at all costs.

First, you should strive for a consistent, medium amount of tongue while kissing. You want the presence of your tongue to be felt, but you don't want to choke her with it. One of my friends was kissing a girl (we were in ninth grade) and he gave her so much tongue that she pulled away dry-heaving. Imagine how he felt while she was bent over, gagging and coughing.

Do not shove your tongue down anyone's throat.

Also, don't transform into a reptile during the kiss. Do not dart your tongue in and out of her mouth. The lizard technique gets you nowhere fast.

Finally, *please* close your eyes once the kiss begins. There's nothing more repulsive than someone staring at you while their tongue is jammed down your throat. It takes all the romance and mystery out of the kiss. And, truthfully, it's a little psycho. Close your eyes, and keep 'em closed till the kiss is over.

When to Call After the First Date

You should wait one day before you call her. Don't call the day after your date, because she'll think that you're too interested in her (at this point she still wants a bit of a chase), and don't wait until day three or you'll come off looking like an asshole. Wait twenty-four hours before calling.

Take It Slow

Once the kissing has begun, don't get nervous and rush through it. The first time my friend "Ike" (we'll call him Ike because his real name is Mike and I wouldn't want to embarrass him by using his real name in a nationally published book) went in to French-kiss a girl, he was in such a hurry that he clanged his teeth against hers.

Ouch!

I have to point out that he was man enough to tell us about it later, and have a good laugh at himself. But save yourself the embarrassment and remember to take it slowly. Savor the moment. Take her in. Smell her scent. Feel her lips. Hear her breathe. It's not a race. When you savor her, she'll know. And she'll like it. Women like to feel appreciated.

The Dating Game

You're learning to master the dating game. Phone calls are like butter. Asking girls out is cake. The good-night kiss doesn't even faze you, because of your confidence. You call her in two days, ask her out again, and it's all gravy. You, my dear Ladies' Man, are dating this girl! Doesn't it feel good? But what happens when things go to the next level?

5
Seeing Girls

"Seeing" a girl means that you've been on several dates and that you've decided to keep dating each other.

A common misconception about seeing a girl is that you have to eventually want to be boyfriend and girlfriend in order to do this.

Personally, just because I'm seeing a girl doesn't mean that I plan on going to the next level of Donkey Kong with her. Just like you can kiss a girl you don't want to date, and date a girl you don't want to see, you can see a girl you don't want to go out with. This is called casual dating, and it can be a beautiful thing.

Many people say that someone is inevitably being led on when two people date with no plans of getting serious, but I think those people are smoking opiates.

Many Ladies' Men (myself included) have gotten into a lot of trouble by sizing a girl up the minute they meet her.

"I'd really like to go out with her."

"Is this meant to be?"

"She could be the one."

"I wonder if that's a push-up bra."

Why do we have to get so serious so quickly? We would be so much more relaxed and better off if we stopped judging every single aspect of a new relationship and started concentrating on enjoying it. The beginning of a relationship is, without a doubt, the best part (except for the whole falling in love and finding a soul mate thing). Nobody has any preconceived notions of the other person, everything is new, and everything can remain positive.

Anytime you can find companionship in another human being, and have an open line of communication about what the both of you want, there's no reason you can't spend time together—going out, hooking up, and hanging out. Every girl you see doesn't have to be the perfect person for you.

I have a problem with wondering whether I'm ever going to find "the one." Many times, I think I would be better off if I learned to live in the moment—to not care about what it's going to be like tomorrow, or the next day, or the next week with this girl.

I need to learn to enjoy *right now*.

What if I started thinking about masturbation the way I think about dating? Imagine the pressure I'd put on myself every time I sat down to jerk off if I thought, "I wonder if this is going to be the best session of spanking it, ever." I'd be disappointed after almost every yank. How can you enjoy anything if you're always waiting for the one time it's going to be perfect?

• • •

So you go on a few dates with a girl, you enjoy her company, you have physical chemistry, but you don't think you want to "go out" with her (i.e., be boyfriend and girlfriend). You *can* continue to see this girl. However, you must let her know that you aren't looking for a serious relationship.

Why?

Because people get emotionally attached—and girls get attached more easily than guys.

Ladies,

Everybody needs to be honest about what they want out of a relationship, *even you.* If you are dating a guy who isn't boyfriend potential, then let him know that you aren't looking for a serious relationship. Don't lead him on. Clear the air.

Also, if a guy says, "I'm just looking to have a good time," or "I'm not looking for a relationship right now," or any of the other lines that we give, then don't try and convince yourself that he'll want to be your boyfriend if you hang around long enough. Don't string yourself along. If you want to be his girlfriend and that's not happening and he is letting you know that it isn't going to happen, then move on. He isn't coming around.

Emotional Attachment

I think this is a basic sociological and biological difference between men and women. Women have a greater capacity to be in touch with their emotions. Their ability is so superior that their physical and emotional lives are inseparable.

Men have a tendency to separate emotion from hooking up. And not only from hooking up, but from most of our lives. We're told that being emotionally distant or bottled up is what it means to be a "man." From the time we're little boys, we are encouraged to equate being emotional with being "womanly." We are encouraged to do everything in our power to avoid being "feminine."

Therefore, expressing our feelings and making them a priority in our lives is a hard thing to do when we're young. After all, it's not "manly."

This is life for most guys.

It's screwed up, but it's life.

It is crucial for us to understand that we have blockages that dam our emotions. Knowing this, we have to consciously fight against it. We have to reclaim that side of our manhood. The side that feels. That cares. That loves. This is one of the greatest struggles and one of the most crucial goals for any true Ladies' Man.

That's right, sensitivity is the essence of being a Ladies' Man. *If you can't be sensitive to your own feelings, it's going to be very hard, if not impossible, to be sensitive to women.* And you are going to hurt a lot of people over the course of your dating life, because you won't be able to validate or understand their emotions.

Let me put this into terms most guys can comprehend:

Ladies,

This is the answer to most of your questions about guys. This is why we don't call when we say we will. This is why we don't open up to you the way we should. This is why, at times, we want out of even the best relationships. This is why we are ready to eat, sleep, shit, and have sex at any time during the day, but will run like hell from having to acknowledge our emotions. Basically, this is why we are so scared of commitment, communication, and love. We seek out situations and people who will *not* force us to feel or listen to our hearts. In short, this is why we're such assholes. Therefore, when you're in a committed relationship, even though it shouldn't be your job, try to show us that it's safe and good to talk about our feelings (and to acknowledge yours). Until that happens, you can pretty much expect the same crap from every guy.

If you're with a Ladies' Man—a guy who is working on becoming more skillful in dealing with his emotions (and yours)—then be kind, understanding, and helpful. However, if you're dealing with the kind of moron who is never going to change (with practice, spotting these guys becomes as easy as spotting fake boobs at the beach), save yourself the heartache and dump his ass right now. Remember that guys are like dogs: There are some you can train and have a happy life with, and others who are going to continue to drink chlorine water and eat their own vomit for the rest of their lives.

You know how pumped up you get in the fourth quarter of a championship game? Let's say it's a basketball game. You're watching the Heat and Lakers on your friend's big-screen TV and they're tied at 100 in double overtime. There are ten seconds left to play and Miami has the ball under their basket with no time-outs left. They give the ball to Dwyane Wade and he's about to pass it in.

He's got Shaq wide open. Shaq goes up—

—and your brother unplugs the TV!

While you're scrambling to get the plug back in the socket, Shaq hits a fadeaway three-point hook shot— just as the clock runs out. In double OT. Of the Finals. You turn the TV back on only to see the champagne bottles popping.

You would be pissed, right? After all, you were emotionally invested in the game.

That's how women feel when their heart enters the relationship—they're emotionally invested. This is especially true if your relationship becomes physical. When you start hooking up, the emotional level gets taken up a notch for the ladies.

Same concept as the Laker/Heat game.

You want to kick the living crap out of your little brother, who's dancing around the room with the plug in his hand screaming, "Neaner, neaner, neaner!" Women want to sucker punch *us* (in the back of the head) when we don't make our intentions known and they become emotionally invested.

What they don't realize is that we're not trying to hurt them.

We're guys.

We're a different breed.

We've been socialized differently.

Despite this, you can avoid incurring the burning hatred of any girl you want to "see" by:

1. **Communicating your intentions clearly.** For example, say something like, "I'm just looking for a ca-

sual relationship right now. I don't want to get in-volved in anything serious and I want you to know that." It's up to her to agree, or take off.

2. **Setting your boundaries very early on.** Boundaries are your line in the sand. They are the set of rules that you post when you enter a relationship, about where you're willing to go, how you want to be treated, how you don't want to be treated, and how much space you need. Honesty and clarity about these issues from the start will alleviate confusion in the future. Learning how to set boundaries is basic training for a Ladies' Man.

I used to be terrible at communicating and setting up my boundaries. Since then I've realized the importance of these two things, and I'm constantly improving. With time, it has gotten easier and easier for me to tell a girl what I want out of a relationship (so that I don't send her mixed signals).

If you tell her what you're thinking regarding your re-lationship (in a wise manner), she can't fault you later, when (and if) you're ready to move on. You've been true to yourself and true to her. And that's pretty much all anyone can ask for.

Social Functions with Girls You're Seeing

The way you introduce the girl you're seeing at social functions is critical: whether you're introducing her to a friend, a family member, or a complete stranger.

Our natural reaction as guys is to say whatever first comes to our minds (superfluous, insensitive, moronic drivel). It's no big deal to us, so we introduce girls how-ever we feel like it. Wrong move. If you do this enough (like I have), you start to realize that you screw up about 50 percent of the time.

Introduction: "This is my girlfriend, Heather."

Right/wrong: Wrong

Why: You shouldn't say this for the most obvious reason—she's not your girlfriend. The two of you are now due for a draining conversation. You're going to have to sit through her saying stuff like, "Oh, I didn't know I was your girlfriend now. If that's the case, how come you don't spend more time with me?"

If you haven't talked about the fact that you two are going out, then you're not going out. And Heather is not (yet) your girlfriend.

Introduction: "This is my friend, Heather."

Right/wrong: Wrong

Why: Go down this path and you are in for a conversation that goes a little something like: "Oh, so now I'm just your friend? What were you trying to do? Keep your options open to meet other women? I didn't know that 'friends' hook up like we do. How many 'friends' like me do you have?"

Don't go there.

Introduction: "This is Heather."

Right/wrong: We have a winner!

Why: Because she *is* Heather. That's her name. She can't get mad about you introducing her by her name. You haven't specified whether she's your girlfriend or not, so people can interpret your introduction in whatever way they choose.

A Ladies' Man secret: Girls are more attracted to guys who are unavailable.

Ladies' Man WARNING: Flirting with other women during a date with Heather is a definite no-no, and a sure way to get a drink thrown in your face. If you are seeing someone, refrain from hitting on women in the presence of your date. You will have opportunities to ask these women out in the future.

Another reason the proper introduction is so important is because there may be some interesting girls at this party. If you're not exclusive with Heather, you may want these ladies to know you're semiavailable. They'll realize that you're on a date with Heather, of course. But they'll also know that she's not your girlfriend. This is exactly how you want to be perceived: as somewhat unavailable.

Breaking the Code: How to Handle the Games Girls Play

Sometimes girls set traps when you're seeing them— tricks that test your seriousness about or commitment to the relationship. They dangle the cheese in the back of the cage and try to ensnare you when you enter for some sharp cheddar. We'll call these traps "games." You have to be on your toes for specific signs when an inadvertent trap is set. I say "inadvertent trap" because most times women aren't setting these traps on purpose. They don't know they're dangling the cheese in the back of the cage.

They're not trying to screw you over. They actually do it because they care. Or because you haven't been clear about where the relationship is going—and they're seeking some enlightenment.

A woman's thought process is much different than a man's. Not better or worse. Different. While a guy would just come out and ask, "Where is this going?" a woman will want to *intuit* where your relationship is headed. This is something a Ladies' Man has to recognize and be sensitive to. Or else he could be entering a world of pain.

The "Hey, It's Me" Game

I'm sitting at home minding my own business one day when the phone rings. I walk over and pick it up,

"Hey, it's me," a girl's soft voice mutters.

"Who the heck is *me*?" I'm thinking.

I have no idea who this girl is, but I'm not about to admit that to her. I don't want her to know that I don't recognize her voice. I could be dating her. My forehead is beading with sweat. How am I gonna get out of this one? I'll try to guess who she is based on the direction of the conversation. I start probing.

"So . . . what did you do today?"

I'm trying to get her to talk about work or school or anything I can pin down. I'm screwed. She's not giving me anything.

"Oh, just the normal routine. You know how it is."

No, I don't know how it is, because I don't know who the hell you are! I can only keep this up for a little while longer because she's on to me.

"Do you even know who this is?" she asks in an annoyed tone.

What this girl is looking for is a sense that she's special to you. She wants you to recognize her voice instantly because it holds an important place in your heart.

Normally I'd spend five minutes in a vague question-and-answer session, trying to deduce who the person on the other end of the phone is, without giving away the fact that I have no clue who she is. But, believe it or not, there is a better way.

When a girl calls and says, "Hey, it's me," you say, "Who's me?" Normally a girl will just laugh, say her name, and continue the conversation.

Deep down she will have gotten the message. You haven't memorized her voice because things between you are just casual.

However, if the girl seems really annoyed that you don't recognize her instantly, try the following:

When she tells you her name, say (in a surprised voice), "Oh, hey! What's up? Are you on a cell phone or something? Your voice sounds so *different*." This gives the impression that you would have recognized her voice UNDER NORMAL CIRCUMSTANCES, but some strange technological glitch has robbed you of the chance to identify her.

Side note: If a girl freaks out on you for not recognizing her voice on the phone it's clear she has greater expectations for this casual relationship than you do. Consider having a serious talk with her about your intentions. Soon.

The "What Are You Thinking Right Now?" Game

This just happened to me with a girl I was seeing. I had my arms around her and was staring at the ceiling deep in thought, when she asked, "What are you thinking right now?"

What kind of question is that? Wouldn't I be talking about what I was thinking if I wanted to share? Yes, I

Ladies,

In all fairness, I ask the "What are you thinking right now?" question in my long-term relationships. Then again, there are many feminine qualities I assume in my relationships—although I draw the line when asked to wear high heels in bed (unless it's Saturday).

would be. But I'm not talking about it, which makes it a thought. *My* thought.

What this woman wants is a deeper look inside your head and your heart. She's hoping that you'll feel safe and secure enough to share your thoughts with her. But what if you're *not* feeling that secure, or what if the content of your thoughts wouldn't exactly make her happy?

Try saying:

"Nothing, I was just spacing out."

She can't fight that, and you get to keep your private thoughts private.

The "What Are We?" Game

A long time ago, I was with this girl, Lara. We had a great casual relationship—and good times together every time we hung out.

But Lara wasn't girlfriend potential. I knew we had no chance long-term. However, women are often thinking about the next level of Donkey Kong.

So I'm lying in bed with her after a hookup, and her voice pierces the silence: "So . . . what are we?"

What this woman wants is to know whether you'd be interested in taking things to a more serious level. She would like a commitment but feels vulnerable about asking for one. (She wants to spur you into "naturally" committing to her by asking this question.)

So she lobs the ball into your court to see what you do with it. How do you handle this game smoothly? First, return the ball. Make her explain.

"What do you mean?" I ask.

Sometimes a woman will back down when faced with having to say something uncomfortable (she wants you to do the work). She'll answer by saying something like, "Oh, never mind."

But she may continue: "I mean, where's this relationship going?"

If you'd like to advance to the next level, by all means, let her know right now. But if you don't want to, I suggest saying something like this:

"We're seeing each other. I'm happy with us right now. We have fun together. We have good conversations. This is what I want out of a relationship. Right where we are. Right here. Right now."

Bam. You've been completely honest. She can either

Ladies' Man WARNING!
Women like to play the "What are we?" game after an orgasm. Why? A man is most truthful postorgasm because his penis won't be doing the thinking for at least another fifteen minutes. However, orgasm or not, where you draw your line in the sand is crucial. You have to draw it and stand firm behind it.

accept your answer or decide that she needs something else. Her answer:

"It's not a big deal. I'm happy too.... Forget I brought it up."

Are we learning?

How to Ensure That It Doesn't Go to the Next Level

If you want to continue seeing a girl and don't see her as girlfriend potential, then you should avoid stepping into dangerous territory blindly. Many of my friends have found themselves in boyfriend land and wondered, "Hey. How the hell did I end up here?"

If you start kissing a girl you're seeing around her friends, your friends, or other people you both know, you are well on your way to going out. How do I know this?

My friend Daves was hooking up with this girl in high school (to avoid causing him utter shame and embarrassment I've cleverly concealed the true identity of my friend by adding an *s* to the end of his name).

Daves knew he didn't want to go out with this girl exclusively. However, it seemed as if she wanted more than just a casual relationship. I advised Daves to evade the *school kiss* at all costs. Once the school kiss is initiated, there's no going back. You don't just kiss a girl one day at school and not kiss her the next day. And if you're kissing every day at school and everyone sees you, then you're definitely going out.

Daves was freaked out because he hugged this girl after fifth-period math every day and he got the feeling that she wanted the kiss. I reminded him that he had to suppress any urge to placate her.

We all had math together, and they always hugged after class in plain view. Since we had been talking about avoiding the school kiss, I decided to watch the hug go down with my friend Mikes.

Daves goes to hug her.

He backs away.

He leaves his hands on her hips (we all know what this means).

They continue to talk as they hold each other.

Mikes and I are watching from about twenty yards away.

"Don't do it, dude." I'm coaching from afar.

"Hang in there, man," Mikes adds in moral support.

She leans in. . . . He leans in. . . . They kiss.

"Goddamn it!" I yell.

"Asshole!" Mikes mutters to himself as he's forced to look away.

Daves walks over to us, slumping as he realizes not only that we saw, but what he's gotten himself into.

"I am such an idiot," he mumbles as he collapses against the wall.

Mikes and I left Daves alone that day, leaning against the wall, to think about what he'd done. And just like that, one of the bravest warriors went down.

The point of this story isn't that you should *never* want to be a girl's boyfriend. The point is that *there are certain girls you will not want to go to the next level with, and it is important for you to draw clear boundaries with these women early on.*

Making Sure It *Does* Go to the Next Level

So let's say you're seeing someone and *you* feel like you want to change the status of your relationship. This situation calls for a delicate balance between showing the girl that you like her and not smothering her. Don't get too serious too quickly. Relax. The beginning of a relationship is a beautiful and rare thing. Enjoy it.

Nothing counts but the present. That's what life is: right here, right now. The worst thing you can do is jump into analyzing whether or not you are "going out" or if she "likes" you or "really likes" you or "really, really likes" you, because you miss the moment when you live in the future.

If you want a girl that you're seeing to become your girlfriend, then treat her better and with more love than you treat anyone in your life. Listen to her, dance with her, eat with her, drive her around shopping, compliment her, bring her thoughtful gifts, and make her laugh. Be as charming as you can be *all the time.* And when you *know* that she wants to be your girlfriend, I urge you to ask her.

I'm old-school. As a traditional man (in an untraditional kind of way), I like formally asking a woman to be my girlfriend.

More important than that, *women* like it.

She may say, "Oh, you didn't have to do all this," when you concoct a loving way to ask her out. She may expect you to act like every other unromantic, inconsiderate guy she's ever dated by doing nothing for her. But this isn't about what women expect from average men; this is about what you should expect of yourself as a Ladies' Man.

A girl doesn't want to become somebody's girlfriend without being able to recall the exact moment her man made it happen. You should make it evident that you would like to take your relationship to the next level by *asking her to be your girlfriend.*

Some of the Benefits of Asking Her to Be Your Girlfriend

1. She'll love you for it.

2. You'll be able to pinpoint your anniversary instead of having to say, "We didn't really have an exact date when we started going out so we just chose one." Can you imagine a married couple saying, "Yeah, we didn't really make a big deal of it or anything. One day I just woke up and asked Bill, 'Are we married now?' And he said, 'Yes.' So we chose June twenty-first as our anniversary because we like that date"?

3. She'll brag to all of her friends, and you'll make their boyfriends look like chumps.

4. You're going to get some serious affection after such a thoughtful gesture.

5. You'll feel good for being romantic and having made your new girlfriend's year.

6. If you grow old with this girl, then someday she'll be telling your grandchildren about what a Ladies' Man you were when you asked her to be your girlfriend.

So *how* should you ask her to be your girlfriend?

There's no right answer, but I'll provide you with some examples of what *could* be done, and you can use them as a model to create your own situation. Choose the scenario you think your girl will like best, then tailor it to her specific tastes:

1. Show up at her house in the morning and make her favorite breakfast. Along with breakfast, give

her a flower and explain to her the ways in which it reminds you of your relationship. (For example, a sunflower can represent the sunshine that her presence brings to your life every day.)

This may sound corny to you, but I can guarantee you that she will love it. If you are too shy to say those kinds of things to her aloud (which is *totally normal*), then write them down in a card. At the end of the card (or after you say it), ask her to be your girlfriend. Let her take your question in, get teary eyed, and hug and kiss you.

2. Take her somewhere scenic like the beach, or the mountains, or the river, or the lake, or the forest, or the desert, or the park. Take her to a place that you know is special to her. After having a great time together at the destination of your choice, give her the letter you wrote her that describes each enchanting facet of her being and your relationship together. (I bet you didn't even know that you wrote a letter!)

While she is reading the letter, hold her. Admire the view. Breathe the fresh air. Talk to her. More importantly, listen to her (all women really want you to do is *listen* to them). At the right moment, take her hand and ask her to be your girlfriend.

3. Prepare a romantic evening. Take her to the nicest restaurant you can afford (make sure they serve food that she enjoys). Be the most chivalrous and thoughtful person you know how to be. Unlock and open her car door for her. Make sure she is comfortably seated before you shut the door. Open every door the two of you encounter and guide her through the threshold. She should always enter first. If you need to cross a street, make sure your hand is on the small of her back, guiding

her safely to your destination. Make her feel protected and taken care of. When you get to your table, pull her chair out and seat her before you sit down. Be charming at dinner. Tell jokes. Make her laugh. Above all, tell her how beautiful she looks. Compliment her. Hold her hand. Go all out on your meal. Get an appetizer, a main course, a drink, and dessert. Eat like a king and treat her like a queen.

When you are done with your evening, go back to one of your homes. (It doesn't matter if you live with your parents. They should be cool with your needing the space to ask her out. Assuming, of course, that they'll believe you when you assure them that you're not going to have unprotected sex with her in your closet or anything.)

Play her favorite CD (you better know what it is), and reveal a gift that you purchased for her. It doesn't have to be expensive; it just has to be pretty and help her to remember how awesome you are. She opens it. She cries. You smile. She hugs you. You ask her to be your girlfriend.

4. You pull out a book.

"A book?" you ask.

"A book," I answer.

Do you know if she has a favorite poet or a favorite author? You should always listen and take notes about things like this when you are in a relationship—you should know her favorite places, her favorite musicians, her favorite books, her favorite foods, her favorite drinks, her favorite flowers, and her favorite movies. These are the things that good boyfriends remember.

Pick a passage from one of her favorite books or an entire poem that reminds you of her. Create a romantic setting (flowers, candles, Nina Simone on the stereo) and read the passage aloud to her. At the end of the passage, take out something that you have written for her, read it aloud, and ask her to be your girlfriend.

What you say will depend on how you feel about her. Your letter could sound something like the following (but don't rip me off word for word because I'll hunt your ass down and slap you across the bank account with a copyright infringement lawsuit). . . .

A Long Love Letter to Your Future Girlfriend

I always wondered how I was supposed to know if I was in love with somebody, because I had never been in love before. Everybody always says that when you are in love you just "know," but if you've never felt something, then how are you supposed to know when you feel it for the first time? I've been in relationships before. I've had crushes on people. I've "liked" people. I've even "really liked" people, but I could never be sure if I was "in love" with them.

Then I met you.

When I'm with you the world around us disappears. Anything is possible and I don't worry as much. Being with you makes me optimistic about my life. When I stare at you I can't look away. Minutes turn into hours with you, and hours turn into days. Mornings fade into afternoons, and afternoons fade into nights.

You make me generous. You make me compassionate. You make me consider *you* before I consider *me*. You've helped me to open up parts of myself that I had never accessed. I am such a better person for having met you.

People always told me that I would "just know" when I was in love.

Then I met you.

And I just knew.

So I would like to ask you, "Will you be my girl-friend?"

You see, ladies, we (guys) aren't that bad. We want to be your boyfriend.

. . .

That's the gist of it. Sure, I'm a romantic, but this letter is just a template to give you an idea of what's possible. However, now that I think about it, maybe such a long letter isn't your style. So here's another letter for you to consider. This one's much shorter but still says everything it should.

A Short Love Letter to Your Future Girlfriend

I planned today for you because I wanted to show you how you make me feel all the time: loved. You are the most special person in my life, and for that reason I want us to make a commitment to each other. Will you be my girlfriend?

. . .

You see, that wasn't so hard, was it? Short, simple, and sweet. And remember that you only get one chance to do this. Don't fuck it up.

6

Girlfriends

"Love is weird."
—MY BROTHER RYAN, AT AGE TWENTY-SEVEN

Earlier you looked inside the Holy Grail and learned the secret to the hearts of young women all around the globe; you have to act like Cool Guy to get girls interested in you. However, once you have a girlfriend, all of these games should stop. It's now time to show your girl what it's like to be with a Ladies' Man.

Ladies' Men treat their girlfriends with complete respect. The games are over (well, most of them anyway). Now show her the *nice guy;* the nice guy is the guy she'll fall in love with (and stay in love with). Unless you engage in one of the . . .

Top Two Ways to Screw Up Your Relationship

The reason I know what *not* to do is because I've done it all.

I've made numerous mistakes in relationships. I've treated women poorly. I've let women treat *me* poorly.

I've screwed the pooch . . . big-time.

So I thought I would save you the time associated with acting like an asshole by letting you learn from my mistakes.

1. Jealous Boyfriend

I used to be a jealous boyfriend (and to some extent, I still am). I couldn't stand the thought of my girlfriend talking to other guys. Why? Because I *am* a guy, and I know what most of us think about all day: women. Primarily, having sex with them.

Most guys—except Ladies' Men—are absolute scum. Period.

There's no disputing it.

I have too many guy friends (and guy friends of guy friends) for anyone to tell me that most guys aren't cavemen dressed in Abercrombie clothing.

Since I knew what guys were really trying to do with my girlfriend, I would get uncontrollably jealous when she hung out with other dudes.

There are two main reasons that guys get jealous. Insecurity and lack of trust.

Insecurity.

Some guys get jealous because they're insecure. They don't think they're good enough for their girlfriend and they can't see why any girl would want to stay with them. Therefore, this type of guy sees plenty of reasons why his girlfriend would want to hook up with other dudes.

I was insecure.

There was always a reason in my mind for her to dump me for someone else. With age, I homed into Cool Guy's frequency and started letting go of my jealousy. I realized that I didn't have any control over my girlfriend.

If she wanted to find another guy, she could find another guy. I learned to let go because I figured out that my girlfriend wasn't a parking space and I wasn't a meter maid.

You can't police your girlfriend's thoughts and actions.

A Ladies' Man doesn't have time to sweat that which he can't control.

And you can't control anybody but yourself.

Think about it. If your girlfriend was constantly nagging you about not cheating on her, would that have any effect on whether or not you *did* cheat? No. If you're going to be unfaithful, then your partner's precautions aren't going to stop you.

The truth is that the more our girlfriends nag us about certain things, the more we want to do them. Well, the same holds true for girls. The more we try to control them because of our fear of their cheating, the more they're going to think about cheating. I should know.

I was friends with this girl who had a controlling boyfriend. He was always scared that she was gonna cheat on him. He pushed her so much to think about it that one night it drove her to me. I was young and foolish (it all happened two hours ago), so I was waiting there for her with open arms. The point is that *you need to stop caring about the things you can't control.* Cool Guy knows that no girl in her right mind would leave him. And if she does, it's her loss.

Remember A.G.B.? He just waits for another door to open.

This is the attitude we want to adopt.

Say it with me: *Making our girlfriends pay for our insecurities is an ugly trait.* There's no reason to think you don't deserve a wonderful girlfriend. When you love yourself enough to have a healthy relationship with yourself, people follow your lead. If you respect yourself, then your girlfriend will too.

And if for some reason she doesn't, you'll have enough self-esteem to dump her and find a woman who will.

Lack of trust.

The other reason guys become jealous is because they don't trust their girlfriend around other guys. This is a no-win situation. If you don't trust your girlfriend around other guys, why are you going out with her? If she's shown you that she'll cheat on you, what's keeping you with her? You may want to consider reevaluating this relationship.

2. Controlling Boyfriend

Being a controlling boyfriend isn't just a bad idea; it borders on abuse (or it can be part of an abusive pattern in a relationship). Chances are you've met a guy like this. You know, the type who soils himself when his girlfriend talks to or spends time with other dudes. Or the guy who tries to control every aspect of his girlfriend's life, so that she's never around other guys. He's a prime example of a controlling boyfriend.

I knew a guy like this in high school. This guy wanted to know where his girlfriend was at *all times*. He started

Ladies,

If you thought your boyfriend was cool and then he suddenly turned controlling and abusive, leave now. If he is acting like a psycho and then apologizing and promising to change and then acting like a psycho and then apologizing and promising to change, you must assume that he will never change (most people don't). You can't be with a guy based on his potential.

freaking out when he hadn't seen or heard from her in a while, calling all of her friends to find out where she was. This psycho even interrupted parties she was at to drag her home, worried that if his girlfriend started to have too much fun with her friends, she was going to find another guy.

So he tried to keep her at his side (or at home when he was out with his friends) 24/7. When his girlfriend wanted to hang out with one of her guy friends, he would lose his shit:

"No way. This guy you want to 'hang out' with just wants to hook up with you!"

"No he doesn't. Casey just wants to be my friend!"

Now, to be fair, I know Casey. Casey probably *does* want to hook up with her. Ninety-nine percent of us have one-track minds. Fuckminds.

But even though the controlling boyfriend has a point, the way he's dealing with his girlfriend is wrong.

If you're ever faced with a situation like this, just say, "Look, I know what this guy wants from you, but if you can't see that, I'll let you find out for yourself."

This creates a win-win situation. If Casey hits on her, she'll know her boyfriend was right all along. She'll respect him for his insight and trust his judgment in the future. If he's wrong, and Casey likes musical theater (and thus just wants to be her friend), he still wins. Because he didn't try to control her.

Cool Boyfriend

Cool Guy has just been resurrected—in boyfriend form.

Cool Boyfriend trusts his girlfriend to deny the guys that try to pick up on her. He doesn't stress about meaningless aspects of his relationship.

However, he also has principles. He can break up with his girl if she isn't treating him the way he deserves to be treated.

Cool Boyfriend gets out of a bad relationship as quickly as he can. He doesn't have time for the useless drama that comes from a relationship that blows.

Cool Boyfriend has a *reciprocal relationship* with his girlfriend. Meaning, it's not one-sided. He has a discussion with his girlfriend and they come to a mutual conclusion about how their relationship will be defined. This includes issues like loyalty and trust. Is the relationship monogamous, or can they see other people? When these boundaries have been set, he kicks back and has fun.

To recap, Cool Boyfriend . . .

1. Doesn't get jealous.

2. Doesn't get mad when his girlfriend spends time with her friends (guys or girls).

3. Doesn't become controlling.

4. Doesn't get abusive.

5. Loves his girlfriend and treats her with dignity and respect.

6. Treats himself with dignity and respect.

Space

For both boyfriends and girlfriends, setting up how much space you need is clutch: space to see your friends, space to see your family, and space to be by yourself. Space gives you the freedom to do whatever you want as a single unit.

Independently.

Space also refers to what kind of sexual activity you're comfortable with. How far is too far for you? Are you okay with public displays of affection? If she grabs your package in front of a bus stop full of senior citizens, will you squirm or smile? Things of that sort.

As soon as you enter into a committed relationship, you should establish how much space you will need to stay happy and healthy.

I don't like feeling like I'm trapped when I'm in a relationship. I don't want to feel like my girlfriend is holding me back from anything. Relationships should open up new worlds for you. When they start closing things off, then I think something has gone wrong.

I like to go to movies by myself.

To go on walks by myself.

To listen to music by myself (like now).

To read by myself (like now).

To write by myself (like now).

To talk to myself (like now).

I love the quiet of being alone. There's nothing more soothing than hearing nothing. Not a peep. In a relationship I try to ensure that I have time for *all* of that. Plus, my alone time helps me appreciate my girlfriend even more—because I've missed her and I'm happy to see her again when my solo time is over.

I know some guys who become so dependent on their partners when they get into relationships that they end up neglecting their friends, their families, or their interests. You need to have other things going on in your life besides your girlfriend. You need to have space.

I had a friend ("had" being the operative word) who was notorious for leaving his friends high and dry for girls. He would be cool with all of the guys when he was single, but as soon as he got a girlfriend, he would drop off the face of the planet.

No calls.

No nothing.

Silence.

Pretty soon this friend didn't have any friends (or at least any good friends) anymore.

I don't want to end up like that.

Her Space

Don't smother your girlfriend. Respect her space the way you want yours to be respected. Giving your girlfriend breathing room works in infinite ways. It gives you time to have your own life and it keeps her interested because you're not chasing her around all day like her puppy dog.

Remember, *people desire those who give them space.*

The Tough Questions

When you're in a boyfriend/girlfriend relationship, two questions are guaranteed to come up. If you don't answer them correctly, you may end up spending *way* too much time in the shower . . . all alone. But don't worry. I'm here to help insure that your hand doesn't get any more exercise than absolutely necessary (and to keep your relationship intact).

Question 1: "Do we *have* to hang out with your friends tonight?"

Cute question. The answer . . .

"Yes!"

Friends are some of the most important people I have in my life. I refuse to compromise my time spent with my friends for anything. I need love and support in my

Ladies,

I'm not being hypocritical here. I am *more than willing* to spend time with my girlfriend's friends—in fact, I enjoy doing so.

life, and my friendships are a great place to give and receive this.

Friendships provide something that a romantic relationship will never provide—a different kind of closeness and understanding. So when your girlfriend tries to ask you, "Do we *have* to hang out with your friends tonight?" you just look her crooked in the eye and say, "Yes. Yes we do."

This is not to say that you shouldn't spend a large amount of alone time with your girlfriend. You *definitely* should. It's just that you *also* have to find room for your friends in your life; you must strike a healthy balance between your friends and your girlfriend.

Question 2: "Does this make me look fat?"

If she doesn't look fat, it's simple: You say, "Of course not, sweetie, you look perfect." However, let's say she does look fat.

You're thinking: It's not the outfit that's making you look fat—it's the fat that's making you look fat.

However, you *do not say this*. What you say is, "Of course not, sweetie, you look perfect."

Why do you say this? Don't question me. Just say it. She'll feel better about herself, and you won't have a crying girlfriend on your hands. Besides, there's no need to add to an already present, nationwide, female weight and appearance complex. Nobody looks perfect all the time. So let's practice:

"Does my butt look big in these jeans?"

"Of course not, sweetie, your butt looks perfect."

"My boobs look really weird in this, don't they?"

"Of course not, sweetie, your boobs look perfect."

Excellent work. Let's move on.

Breaking Up

If someone isn't treating you right or if you're unhappy in your relationship, then it's time to get out the metaphorical boot. The best policy with breaking up is to rely on good old-fashioned honesty. Tell her the truth. Whatever you feel. You'll feel better if you're honest with her. You just have to *nut up* and do it. (I am my ex-coach's excess testosterone.)

However, if total honesty isn't your cup of green tea yet, then you might want to think about . . .

The Friend Talk

Giving the friend talk never fails. Whether it's genuine or a harmless lie, it doesn't matter. Just tell her:

"I don't know if I have time for a romantic relationship in my life right now, but I know that I want to keep you as a friend. I'm sorry, but I think it's better this way, because I don't want to screw up our friendship."

Women can't fight this. You've paid them the ultimate respect by saying that you want to stay friends.

The friend talk is undefeatable.

Let's face it, women aren't stupid. In fact, they're way smarter than you. They know they're getting dumped when you give them the friend talk. It's just a courteous way to let them down softly. In the words of my friend Mikes, the friend talk "is a classy move."

At the heart of it, breaking up is about telling the least offensive truth, making it possible to skate out of the relationship without getting slammed into the boards. The friend talk is one version of the least offensive truth. When you give the friend talk, you don't say to what extent you want to remain friends. Perhaps you are implying distant friendship in which you will check in with her every six months . . . or every six years.

You're not lying.

You're telling the least offensive truth.

For instance, you could be breaking up with your girlfriend because she shits in her sleep and you don't like going to the dry cleaners every morning. Instead of humiliating her by telling her that blowing mud during the wee hours of the night is a deal-breaker, you give the friend talk.

Understand?

And if you *do* want to remain good friends with her, make the effort.

The friend talk never fails.

How to Break Up

Mode: By phone

Right/wrong: Wrong

Why: The phone breakup is a low-class move. It's the coward's way out. If you're going to break up with your girlfriend, then you need to have the decency to do it in person. You can't dump a girl over the phone.

Mode: E-mail

Right/wrong: Wrong

Why: This is even worse than the phone breakup and requires even less balls (maybe even *negative balls*). Breaking up with someone via e-mail is like having an online funeral. Be a Ladies' Man. Do it in person.

Mode: Instant Messenger

Right/wrong: Wrong

Why: I don't even want to believe that anyone would consider breaking up with someone over IM. One last time: Do it in person.

How to Know When It's Over

In your tenure with women you're going to have to break up with many girls—girls you're dating, girls you're seeing, and girls you're going out with. The keys to a smooth breakup are:

1. Being 100 percent sure that you are through with the relationship. Breaking up causes irreparable damage that can make it hard, if not impossible, to get back together without resenting the hell out of each other.

2. Getting out *as soon as possible* once you are absolutely positive that you have found a woman's *fatal flaw*.

The *fatal flaw* is any aspect of a woman's character that makes her undateable. My list of *fatal flaws:*
She's dumb.
She's racist.
She's homophobic.
She plays head games.

All of these character traits are deal-breakers for me. That's exactly what the fatal flaw is: the deal-breaker. The part of a girl that you could *never* tolerate.

We all have imperfections. However, a fatal flaw isn't an imperfection. A fatal flaw is what it sounds like: fatal. Not getoverable.

From the moment you encounter the fatal flaw (and are 100 percent certain that it's fatal), you have twenty-four hours to get out of the relationship.

Don't fight it.

Save yourself the time and heartache of dragging out a relationship that's been doomed for months. When you become aware of her fatal flaw or fatal flaws, abort mission.

Save yourself and your principles while you can.

When It's Not Over

If you are just partly sure that your relationship isn't going to work, my advice is to hold off on the dumping. Wouldn't you rather spend a couple extra days examining the relationship than ending something too early that could have functioned beautifully through mutual change and mindful effort?

Contrary to what many people believe in today's day and age, *relationships are not all fun and games; relationships are often hard work.* You should meditate on the current state of your relationship to determine whether you are contemplating ending it for a valid reason, or whether you are thinking of leaving because you are immature, shortsighted, and wouldn't mind being able to hook up with a girl who isn't your girlfriend. (It's okay, we've all been there.) If you suspect your impulse is the result of any of those issues, think about giving your relationship another try—this time with more of an open mind.

PART 3

Sex/Hooking Up

In this part of the book I'm going to pass down some helpful information about sex. You will learn about copping a feel, taking off a girl's bra, vaginas, "fingering" (or manually stimulating) a girl, "going down" (performing oral sex) on a girl, female orgasms, the G-spot, hand jobs, blow jobs, intercourse, and finally, every guy's favorite sexual subject . . . impotence (*the inability to get a boner*).

Most guys I know get advice about sex from their friends. I'll let you in on a little secret: **The majority of your friends don't know any more about sex than you do.**

You'd be better off listening to a dog about hooking up than listening to your buddy (even though sometimes the similarities are striking). Think about it: Dogs get a lot more action than most guys. Then again, it's much easier for dogs; it's just, "Hey, I've got a doggy boner with lipstick attachment and you're in heat, so let's bone."

If you have cool parents, you *can* and *should* go to them for information about sex. However, most young guys don't have a relationship with their parents that's open enough to ask about doing it "doggy style." Furthermore, your parents might not feel that your questions about sex are appropriate. And let's face it, talking to your parents about sex can be *really* uncomfortable.

In this section of the book I've included a giant drawing of a vagina (it is not drawn to scale; well, maybe it is for some women) so that you can get acquainted with the female body. Then we'll get down to the good stuff—how to please, and be pleased by, women.

7

Pleasuring Your Girl

What does it mean to "lose your virginity"?

It sounds like a stupid question, right? It's actually a difficult and important question to answer. For most guys, losing your virginity is thought of as the first time your penis enters a vagina. And for women, the first time a penis enters *their* vagina.

That definition is suspect.

In my opinion, it is limited and incorrect to say that sexual penetration is the only way to determine a woman's or man's virginal status.

First of all, it's a well-documented fact that the Clitoris—not the vaginal opening—is the sexual epicenter of a woman's body. We know that to have orgasms a woman needs to have her Clitoris stimulated.

Furthermore, we know that the Clitoris receives minimal stimulation in most intercourse positions (the way we commonly measure the losing of one's virginity).

When oral and many other forms of sex provide greater pleasure and satisfaction for women, why is the one act (penetration) that provides them with the least pleasure and the most issues used to define their passage into adulthood?

Besides this, oral sex is often more pleasurable for men than sexual intercourse. Therefore, measuring a man's virginal status according to whether or not he's had sexual intercourse is just as ludicrous (not Ludacris) as doing so for women.

I've got an idea.

What if we started to define the loss of a man's and woman's virginity by the first time they achieved an orgasm with a partner? I can tell you one thing: We would encounter millions of women who have been having "sex" their whole lives who are still virgins. We'd also find a lot of folks who thought they were virgins who really aren't.

Maybe this new way of defining virginity could provide some growth in sexual relationships. Many men in today's world want to devirginize every woman they encounter by having sex with her. Those same guys in my imaginary world (Colin's World) would want to be the first guy to bring a woman to orgasm. This way, the focus of sexual interaction would be to give a woman her first orgasm.

Some call me a revolutionary.

This would also reduce STD risks and undesired pregnancies. Why? Because a man's only goal in life wouldn't be to shove his penis in the first consenting vagina he encounters.

My view regarding sex and virginity would reduce a lot of pressure and prevent a lot of warts. You wouldn't have to take on responsibilities that you're not ready for (i.e., getting a girl pregnant) just to lose your virginity. You could lose your virginity by receiving a hand job (lower-risk) and your girlfriend could lose her virginity by you fingering her (given that she has an orgasm).

I don't know about you, but I like this idea. Every Ladies' Man should think about adopting it as his own.

So, with that in mind, let's talk about the ways that you and your girlfriend can please each other—without having intercourse.

Pleasing Your Girl

The sexual goal of every Ladies' Man is to please his woman, whether that means helping her have one orgasm, multiple orgasms, or doing nothing to her. The primary sexual focus of a Ladies' Man is to make the woman he's with feel great about her mind and her body.

A Ladies' Man is a spiritual leader whose lifelong ambition is to pleasure women.

What kind of Ladies' Man would Gandhi have been (he actually likes me to call him "O.G.")? A nonviolent giver, that's what kind. Give, give, give, give, give. This is your job.

O.G. knew what was up.

You, my fellow Ladies' Men, were put on this planet to address the problems that other guys have created for women.

Other guys have made women feel neglected. You'll make them feel cherished.

Other guys have kissed them wrong. You'll kiss them right.

Other guys have touched them wrong, licked them wrong. You won't.

Other guys have failed to help them reach orgasm. You won't (you definitely won't).

Lastly, other guys have tarnished the reputation of Ladies' Men all around the world.

You won't.

You, as a Ladies' Man, realize that a woman's pleasure and satisfaction come above all else. It's not about you. It's about her. You'll show her how wonderful she is by showing her how wonderful you can make her feel.

Communicating in Bed

When you are in a loving, committed, long-term relationship, the best way to learn what your girlfriend wants in bed is to *ask her*.

Great sex comes from communicating (or from being with me).

In other words, she tells you what feels good to her, and you tell her what feels good to you. Then you branch out and experiment from that base of knowledge about your partner's desires.

Don't assume you'll know what feels good to her. Each woman is unique. (And besides, there might be some freaky ass thing she wants you to do to her that she's been too embarrassed to ask you for.)

Good communication is why guys have more enjoyable sex with girlfriends than with random partners. Listening to and learning from women about their sexual desires will make you more attentive to all female needs.

But if your girlfriend is sexually ignorant, she may have no idea what she wants. That's where I come in. I'm going to help you become **the man** in bed.

Marathon Kissing

Kissing is sexy, it's fun, and it gets the juices flowing. *Marathon kissing*, however, is not good.

Marathon kissing is when you continue to kiss and kiss and kiss because neither of you is sure if it's going any further (i.e., if you're going to get naked). So you both keep kissing and waiting. Kissing and waiting.

It just gets old.

You have a couple of choices when you catch yourself falling into this trap; you can try to bring the hookup to the next level, or you can take a break and end the session. So let's talk about kicking this up a notch. . . .

Copping a Feel/Taking Off the Bra

If you can tell that she wants to take the hookup further, your next move is to get her turned on by rubbing the right parts of her body (on the outside of her clothes). You want her to feel like she's with a man, not a boy. So take your time. Don't dive right under her shirt. Caress her everywhere. Rub her stomach, her back, her thighs, her butt.

It's a good idea to kiss her all over while you are caressing her body. Kiss her neck. Her cheeks. Lick her ears. Kiss her arms. If you know that the hookup is going to get serious—i.e., if she's communicated this to you in some blatant manner—then you can graze her vagina on the outside of her clothing (we'll cover this in more detail in a second).

So you're rubbing, and she's breathing heavily, and you know that the next move is to take off her bra.

I was always scared that I wasn't going to be able to get a girl's bra off. I didn't have any idea how it unhooked. In fact, I didn't even know it had hooks. Bras

Ladies,

   If you know that the hookup is going to the next level, help us out and take off your bra. It's sexy when a girl takes off her bra for a guy.

terrified me. I have friends to this day who still have trouble with them.

Namely . . . me.

It may be a bit gross, but there *is* something you can do to practice taking off bras. You can practice with the bra of someone in your house. (Like your mom's or your sister's.) It's not really practicing; it's more like studying. You study to find out if they have hooks, if they unhook in the front or back, what kinds of different bras exist, and so on.

And please don't practice with your mom's bra while the bra is on. I'm talking about taking a bra from her drawer and examining it. It sounds pathetic, but it's better than being in the moment and struggling for five minutes to get a girl's bra off. *That's* pathetic.

Girls like to feel like guys know what they're doing.

It makes girls feel comfortable.

I know this all sounds hard, but if you can stay confident, you will be rewarded.

In most cases, you should assume that the bra unhooks in the back. If you reach back and find nothing there, then you know it must unhook in the front— between her boobs.

The truth is that if you're with a cool girl, and you're struggling, she'll take off her bra before you have a mental breakdown. But if this doesn't happen, feel free to ask her to take off her bra.

Say, "Do you feel comfortable with taking off your bra?"

Women and Body Image

In all instances, you have to be mindful of a woman's apprehensions and insecurities. Guys are told that it's okay to come in all different shapes and sizes. Girls are not given this same luxury in our society. Girls are told that they have to be skinny and have big breasts. By magazines. By TV. By film. By radio. By most men. By most women. Can you imagine how damaging that is? Look at popular media outlets and the impossible standards they set for women. It's bullshit! It's messed up, and it's a major reason why women—women of all ages—have complexes about their looks. Women aren't preoccupied with body image just because they're women. It's not female nature; it's a response to society's messages.

Chew on this: Barbie has programmed generations of girls to want to look tall, skinny, blonde, and big-breasted. Barbie has represented the "perfect woman" for many women. However, upon examination of Barbie's proportions (height, waist size, breast size, etc.), smart people who know how to add and subtract determined that if Barbie were a real woman, she would not be able to stand up straight. Her breasts are so big in proportion to her waist and height that her body would not be able to support itself. She would literally fall head over heels. Barbie is so "perfect" that she would resemble Quasimodo if she were a real woman.

Now let's take a look at Ken. Ken's crotch is flat, like a flapjack. I'm talking no package. What do you think would have happened to you if Ken had come equipped with a penis the size of a telephone pole? What kind of body image would we have?

Remember: A little sensitivity goes a long way.

Don't say, "Take off your bra!"

This isn't a stickup. She has a large say in the matter.

You also don't want to say, "Would you care to take off your bra, because I would really enjoy sucking on some boobies right now."

That's the Human Boner again. Remember, Cool Guy.

As always, you have to be sensitive to your woman's feelings. If she says she doesn't want to take her bra off, then back off. It's her decision and it's not going to kill you to stay away from her chest.

See, a girl's chest can be a touchy subject, regardless of the size of her breasts.

In my experience, I've found that the smaller the breasts, the more insecure the girl. So be prepared to give a little more space if you're hooking up with a girl who has smaller boobs. Be delicate. Be understanding.

Imagine if we had to wear our dicks on our foreheads and everyone we walked by commented on them. That would be pretty embarrassing for some of us, wouldn't it? (*Not* for me, of course.) Especially if it was cold out.

Long story short: Some girls will want to keep their bras on during the hookup. It's not the ideal situation for you, but you'll just have to deal with it.

"Heavy Petting"

Oh my God! You got the bra off! Congratulations!

You feel like a church choir should start singing, "Ha-le-lu-jah! Ha-le-lu-jah! Ha-le-lu-jah!"

As is key in all aspects of hooking up, do not get too excited too fast. Don't grab at everything all at once. (It's not your seventh birthday party. At least I hope not. She's not a piñata, and the candy's not going any-where.)

Take your time and play it cool.

Caress her body. *All* of her body, not just the parts that *you* want to touch. Lay off the breasts and the crotch for a while. You'll be surprised which parts of a woman's body can turn her on. Remember that physical pleasure is specific to each girl. Be attentive to what she responds to. You can judge her response by listening to her breathing and sensing how and where she is moving her body. Is her breathing getting heavier, sexier, and more excited when you do certain things to her? When you touch a specific body part, is she moving it closer to you, or is she slightly pulling that part of her body away from you? Be present.

Now she's comfortable with you, so you can start to caress other places. Caress her breasts. Don't tug, pull, yank, or squeeze! Unless she asks you to, in which case you must willingly oblige (it's a tough job, but some-body's gotta do it).

Remember that girls, like guys, are in a supersensitive state when they're aroused. If she doesn't tell you other-wise, be soft. Play with her nipples.

By the way, don't be shocked to see girls with com-pletely different types of nipples. Nipples, much like breasts, come in all shapes and sizes. The nipples can be a huge turn-on. Don't pinch them or squeeze hard. (How would you like one of your balls squeezed or pinched when you're horny?)

After you've caressed her breasts, maybe you want to lick her nipples. Don't bite! (Unless asked to.) Lick softly at first and gauge how intense she likes her licking. Lis-ten to her breathing and feel her body.

Now you're ready to begin kissing again. Kiss her stomach. Go down farther. . . . No, no, farther than that, and kiss her inner thighs. This is an erogenous zone. Maybe you want to tease her and blow on her vagina.

When I say "blow on her vagina," I mean blow on it while her panties are still on. And blow lightly; you're not trying to put out a fire.

She should now be relaxed and aroused. Goal accomplished. In her eyes, you're a sensitive love machine. In your eyes, and the eyes of the omniscient one (me), you're a Ladies' Man. You've played it cool up to this point. You've shown her that you're a good kisser, you've savored each moment, and you've made it clear that you are there to please her. You're in no hurry to slobber all over her body and whip your dick out. You're not one of those horny, sweaty, gross guys who have no idea how to hook up. She knows that you've been here before and that you'll be here again.

Now in some cases I think the best move here is to stop hooking up with her.

I know most of you guys are thinking, "What? You can't stop here, dude!"

Yes, you can. It's respectful to stop here. You've had fun. You've learned a little more about hooking up and being with a different girl. And most of all, she thinks you're a stud. You're sweet. You're sensitive. You're a great hookup. And she knows that you're not just trying to sleep with her.

If you care about this girl or you think that you might want to have her as a consistent hookup, stopping can guarantee future action (or a future relationship). By stopping now, you don't make her uncomfortable by going too fast. And you can guarantee that she will want more.

How could she not want more?

With that said, if you *both* want to get it a little more

heated, then you have my blessing. If she's *absolutely 100 percent* ready for you to go further and she *tells* you that, then it's on like Donkey Kong.

But if you sense that she's unsure *even in the slightest,* you should start massaging her back and then tell her you just want to lie there with her.

She'll fall in love as soon as you say that. "I just want to hold you." It sounds cheesy, but for me it's often the truth. Sometimes I would rather talk all night and then fall asleep holding my girl. I love that.

Stopping also ensures anticipation; it keeps the mystery in your relationship. Sometimes if you go too far with a girl too quickly, you can end up losing interest in her.

Besides all this, *you* may not feel ready or be comfortable with going any further. Despite what your friends might tell you, this is a *totally normal* feeling. It has happened to me many times.

Just because you're a guy doesn't mean you can't stop the hookup—even if she wants to go further.

Moving too fast can make someone regret something. You don't need to accomplish everything in bed *right now*. There's plenty of time. Hooking up will always be a possibility, but your innocence is not something that will always be attainable.

So go run Mushroom Tip Rich under some cold water and cool off.

Kissing and Telling

My dad gave me this advice and I never forgot it: **A true gentleman never kisses and tells.** There is nothing worse than a guy who feels like he has to brag about hooking up.

It's important to share your experiences with one or

two trustworthy friends in order to learn from them, but keep it between your best friends and your girl. Trust me, she'll appreciate it. And so will you.

Don't brag to your buddies in the locker room and start talking about how you "boned her and she loved it." It's a low-class move. Plus it will start the rumor mill at a woman's expense.

Keep your mouth shut.

Reality Check

Most girls who are brought to the physical and emotional state that I previously described will, sooner or later, want you to continue pleasuring them. So for those of you who think you're ready for candy land, I give you . . .

Giving a Girl an Orgasm

Orgasms are the key to your sexual subsistence.

Not *your* orgasms.

Her orgasms.

The road to the female orgasm goes through the heart and the Clitoris.

So help her to have one.

Or two.

Or three.

A girl will orgasm only when she is comfortable with herself *and* with you. Therefore, before you begin to touch her, your job is to ensure her solace and her peace of mind.

Relaxation and comfort need to be present both physically and emotionally. Physical comfort stems from massaging, heavy petting, and kissing. You know how to do all of these things.

Emotional relaxation is derived from how you treat her, the way you talk to her, the things you do for her, and so on—you've also learned how to succeed at this.

Beyond emotional and physical trust, there's one pertinent word that is essential to orgasmic pleasure for women: *Clitoris!* Your job is to stimulate her Clitoris until she's ready to explode with pleasure.

Fingering

Most of you have heard of using your fingers to play with a girl, right? This is known as "manual stimulation" or "fingering."

Before I begin my instruction on this, I want to point out that there are *many* ways to finger a girl. I will not be covering *every way,* because my goal is only to lay out a sexual framework for you—a framework that you can use to discover things for yourself. (Plus, I'm a shrewd businessman and I'm saving the really freaky stuff for the follow-up book: *A New Ladies' Man: A Detailed Guide to Sex.*)

So I will give you one way, a good way, to please a girl with your hand. Here it is—your standard technique for fingering:

You've already done some heavy petting and **she has made it clear to you that she wants to take things to the next level.** It's go time.

Start off by lightly running your fingers all around her thighs. Let your fingers barely touch her vagina a couple of times. (Teasing is a key factor in turning women on.) This will get her wet if she isn't wet already from your previous petting session.

A girl gets "wet" when the vagina secretes liquid. This liquid is meant for lubrication when a woman gets turned on. Getting her wet is key. The fluid produced will help your fingers slide around her vagina in a desirable fashion.

You may have to get your fingers wet by touching her vaginal opening (the hole where the liquid is produced) so that you can bring the lubricant up to her Clitoris (if the entire place isn't already drenched, which it could be).

Now she's dying for you to play with her. However, you should always hold out on the actual fingering for at least a minute longer than you think you should. Anticipation is a huge turn-on.

A Clit a Day Keeps the Doctor Away

The Clitoris is your key to Ladies' Man land.

If you don't know what a Clitoris is, you need to become well acquainted with one. It sounds like I'm suggesting having a cup of coffee with a Clitoris. (To let you know, I have capitalized the word *Clitoris* throughout the book.)

The Clitoris has a buttload of nerve endings, kind of like a guy's penis tip. (Actually, a Citoris has twice the amount of nerve endings that your penis tip does, and a Clitoris's only purpose is pleasure.) That should give you a clear indication of how sensitive to be with a woman's Clit.

There's no bigger turn-off for a girl than having a guy brutalize her Clitoris and be totally clueless about it. As a Ladies' Man, you need to master the Clitoris, revere the Clitoris, and love the Clitoris.

The Clitoris is located above the vaginal opening (the hole), right where the inner lips meet (where they come to a point right below the majority of a girl's pubic hair). NOTE: THIS IS *NOWHERE NEAR THE OPENING OF THE VAGINA*; it's about an inch above it.

The Clitoris is usually the shape of a small pea (nobody said this was going to be easy) and to top off the small size, a Clitoral hood often covers the Clitoris. The Clitoral hood is exactly what it sounds like; a little piece of skin covering the Clit.

Like a hood for a sweatshirt.

If you know what the Clitoris is and where to find it, then you're ready to proceed but if you don't, you need to do some research.

Give Her a Hand

Since most people hook up with the lights off, you need to be able to locate the Clitoris by touch, not by sight. Very rarely are you going to be staring at a woman's vagina while wearing a miner's helmet. (And if you *are* using one of those helmets, then you're into some pretty freaky shit.)

I have a suggestion. If it's dark and you're unsure exactly where her Clitoris is, use anywhere up to four fingers to gently move around the entire vaginal area in a

Ladies,

This is a great time during the hookup for you to guide the guy's hand to your Clitoris. This way, you eliminate the potential for error. You can even circulate his hand on your Clit, thereby showing him precisely how you want it done. Guys do not have a problem with guidance. We like it. A self-assured woman in bed is sexy.

circular motion. This way you cut down the chances of missing her Clit—and annoying her by rubbing some part of her vagina that is not stimulating her.

However, if you *do* know where her Clitoris is, then I suggest rubbing it with the two fingers in between your pinky and your pointer finger. You can keep the Clit in between your fingers for some of the circular rubbing and keep it directly on your middle finger for the other portion of the rubdown. This is a nice way to vary what she's feeling.

If you can't find her Clitoris, by all means ask her where it feels good. You don't want to be striking out while she's too scared to grab your hand and put it in the right place. (If you're lucky, you'll be with a girl who *will* speak up. But no matter what, you may need to get her to tell you how she feels.)

A Reminder About Talking During Sex

While I have stressed that it is a good idea to feel comfortable enough to communicate with your partner, talking *too* much is a huge turn-off. **You're hooking up, not having a conversation.** And when you do talk or ask her a question, you don't want to sound clueless or lost. Don't be a dumb-ass. Don't say, "Excuse me, I was wondering where I could find your Clitoris." You need to remember Cool Guy.

Focus the question on her. Say things like, "Where do you like it?" "Does that feel good?" "Do you like that?" (This is hot and implies that you know what feels good for *other* girls. You just want to find out what specifically feels good for *this* girl.)

Ask in a sexy way. Almost like you're talking dirty.

The goal is to eventually *not* have to ask *any* questions, because you will be able to sense what she wants without having to open your mouth. When this happens, you've become a Jedi Master of sexual pleasure. So you either played it super-cool and knew where her Clitoris was, or you asked her and she guided you there. Either way, you're the man.

You're gently rubbing her Clit in circular motions with one or two fingers. Continue to rub while I digress.

Don't Believe the Hype

Most guys are under the impression that fingering a girl involves sticking their fingers in and out of her vagina like a penis during penetration. I have news for you: **Most women do not climax (have orgasms) during penetration of any kind.**

So jamming your finger in and out of her vagina is just going to frustrate her, piss her off, and make her certain that you're an idiot. (Even though she might act like she likes it—either because she wants to please you or because she *thinks* she should like it.)

It won't give her an orgasm.

Just so we're clear: Do not stick your fingers in and out of her vagina unless she asks you to, *and* unless it's in conjunction with rubbing her Clitoris (but we'll get to that in a second).

So you've been rubbing her Clit in circular motions the whole time I've been talking about the golden rule of fingering. You want to start out slow and get progressively more intense (*slightly* harder, *slightly* faster) as the fingering continues.

Keep in mind that you may need to switch hands, because unlike most guys, it takes girls a long time to climax. (It could be ten, twenty, or even thirty minutes!) Your wrist or hand may cramp up. Sometimes you have to play through the pain, but it helps to become ambidextrous—*equally skilled with both hands.* Switch hands if one cramps up in battle.

Keep It Clean, Keep It Safe

Guys, if you are in a sexual relationship or plan to be in the near future, then you must keep your finger-nails trimmed and your hands clean. A ragged or long nail can cause a woman discomfort when you are fin-gering her. And if a woman is in a state of discomfort while hooking up with you, then she won't be comin' back for more. Make sure your hands are clean as well. A dirty hand could lead to an infection for the woman you're with—and if a girl walks away from your hookup with an infection, you will not be getting another call from her any time soon.

As she starts to get more excited, apply a *little* more pressure and go a *little* faster.

With time, you should be able to tell how close a girl is to climaxing. If you feel that she is a couple minutes from having an orgasm, begin going even faster (just a little) and apply more pressure (just a little).

This Little Piggy Went to the Market, and This Little Piggy Went to . . .

Now you have a decision to make: You can either keep rubbing her Clitoris in the same fashion until she has an orgasm (this *will* do the trick) or, when you feel her about thirty seconds to a minute away from climaxing, you can place one, two, or three fingers inside her. (The number of fingers you choose should depend on the girl, your experience together, and the size of the space you're working with. If she's inexperienced, you only want to use one finger. Otherwise, you may cause her pain.)

To go with option number two, insert one (or more) of the fingers on your off hand, keeping your palm facing the ceiling. Keep in mind that the most sensitve (and thus most easily aroused) part of the inside of the vagina is the first couple of inches. So shoving your fingers deep inside a girl isn't going to do anything but possibly hurt her. (You only need to insert your finger to somewhere around your second knuckle.)

Now, begin moving your fingers as if you're telling someone to "come here."

With the "come here" movement, your fingers are hitting the upper wall of her vagina (G-spot), which is usually denser with nerve endings than the rest of the vagina.

Continue to rub her Clit in circular motions while keeping the "come here" motion with your off hand. This takes coordination. It's like patting your head with one hand and rubbing your stomach with the other.

However, if you are doing this correctly, right about now, she should be having a pretty spectacular orgasm.

V-Day

There's no feeling in the world like bringing a girl to orgasm—especially if your woman isn't used to guys. making her climax (which most aren't).

If you have listened well and followed orders, your woman will be pleased, and you will be well on your way to obtaining the sexual prowess of a Ladies' Man.

Remember that there is no guarantee that your girl will have an orgasm. Don't feel like a loser if she doesn't. She might need to trust you a bit more before she'll allow herself to orgasm. Just take all the steps you can to pleasure her as much as possible and you've won the battle.

Ladies' Man WARNING: Some women do not enjoy simultaneous Clitoral and vaginal stimulation. For certain women it is "too much" to deal with all at once. So if you don't know whether your girlfriend can handle the two-hand technique, it is a safer move to stay on the outside of her vagina by rubbing her Clit in circular motions until she has an orgasm. If you are unsure how your girlfriend feels about the simultaneous stimulation, talk to her about it before you hook up again.

Ms. Clean

Contrary to popular belief (and unlike the penis), the vagina is a self-cleaning organ. Not only is the vagina self-cleaning on a daily basis, but it's even more so during sexual stimulation. When girls get wet, it's not just for lube. The liquid secreted is for cleaning. That means that a woman's vagina is cleaner when she's sexually aroused.

However, despite the fact that it's clean, it's completely normal for her vagina to have a scent. If you're diametrically opposed to any sort of smell, make sure you both shower before you hook up. Lots of guys, on the other hand, like me, enjoy the scent.

Don't be scared of the vagina.

Embrace the vagina.

Don't fight the vagina.

Love the vagina.

Going Down on Girls

Oral sex and your woman. It's simple: You gotta do it! Why? Because she'll love it.

I must point out that you shouldn't be sticking your tongue into every vagina you encounter. It's not safe. By *not safe,* I mean that *you can contract a sexually transmitted disease* from performing oral sex on a woman. That's why you have to save the downtown fox-trot for those girls that you truly care about: girlfriends or girls you've been dating for a *long* time.

Before I tell you how to perform oral sex, consider this. . . .

About Oral Sex

How is conventional sex defined in today's world? By the penis penetrating the vagina in the missionary position (girl on the bottom, guy on top).

Why is conventional sex characterized by the missionary position? Because much of the world revolves around male pleasure.

Most women get little or no pleasure from sex in the missionary position (besides the pleasure of pleasing their man).

If the world were run by women, oral sex would be considered "conventional sex." Why? Because it ensures that a woman has an orgasm pretty much every time she has sex.

And the switch to oral sex isn't solely about female pleasure. Men can, at times, be avid advocates of the blow job over the old humperoosky.

So what is a Ladies' Man to do?

You can make sure that the women you hook up with are pleasured in less "conventional" ways—for instance,

Ladies,

If your man isn't yet sexually skilled or in tune with your mind and body enough to help you achieve an orgasm, then don't be afraid to replace his hand with yours and finish yourself off. Take over with your finger and ask him to hold you close and whisper into your ear—he can talk dirty to you, he can talk sweetly to you, or he can masturbate in front of you while you're on your way to making yourself come. Use your imagination. Just don't be afraid to pleasure yourself. You don't want the hookup to end without you getting off.

by going down on your woman and making sure that you do all you can to bring her to orgasm.

Nothing less.

I would like to make clear that I have nothing against conventional sex (i.e., penetration in the missionary or any other position). It can be a wonderful way of achieving a specific type of closeness. If you're part of a lucky, *very* small percentage of men, you can even make your partner climax during penetration. But women need more stimulation than is commonly received during most acts of penetration. To rely on penetration alone as your way of having sex makes you a bad lover.

A Ladies' Man makes sure that his female partner is receiving equal pleasure. Meaning, she has an orgasm too.

Performing Oral Sex

If you want to go down on her right after the heavy-petting stage, then begin by kissing her stomach. (Again, read the signs to be sure she's giving you the go-ahead. If you get the slightest inclination that she's not ready for oral sex, return to our lesson on fingering.)

Kiss all around her stomach and then start kissing downward toward her vagina. Kiss right above her vagina and then proceed down even farther to her thighs. Kiss her inner thighs (close to her vagina). Blow on her vagina to tease her.

Once again, take your time. Just because I go through the routine in a paragraph doesn't mean it should only take you thirty seconds.

You might want to lightly lick her vagina once and then go back to her thighs. **You want her begging for it before you start.** Once you're ready to begin, then you need to locate her Clitoris, either with your tongue or your finger. If it's easier to find her Clit with your finger, then find it, hold your finger on it as a place marker, and then let your tongue take the place of your finger.

Ladies,

When a guy's tongue hits the perfect spot and starts moving in just the right way, let him know. Tell him, "Yeah, right there. Just like that! Keep licking it just like that!" It's sexy, it will turn him on, encourage him, and it will guarantee that he won't start a different, less satisfying motion.

When going down on a girl, you follow the same principles as fingering, except you do it all with your tongue. You should lick her in circular motions, although you can also switch it up by licking the Clitoris up and down, sideways, and by continuously flicking it with your tongue. Experiment by licking her Clit with different parts of your tongue, as each part produces a different effect.

Do not bite her Clitoris! This is like a girl biting your penis tip when she's giving you a blow job. Not a very appealing thought, right? The Clit is sensitive enough. It does not need to be bitten. Ever.

Keep in mind that, like your hand, your mouth might get tired along the way—this is when you can take over with your hand for a while. Girls should do the same thing with guys. It allows the jaw to relax, and then you can go back at it.

Like I said, apply the same principles as fingering. Keep licking until you feel that she's about a minute away from an orgasm. Then decide whether you want to put a finger or two inside of her, or if you want to just continue licking her until she comes.

If you're not intimately familiar with the fact that she likes a finger or two inside her, then I would suggest keeping your hands to yourself and just continuing to use your mouth until she has an orgasm.

Give yourself a hand at this point. Your mission is complete.

You have to learn to love going down on girls.

It's not just a job.

It's a way of life.

I would like to stress that in giving you an example of how to finger a woman and how to go down on a woman, I have provided you with *only two* examples of how to help a girl have an orgasm. There are many others ways to satisfy a woman sexually that are not covered in this book. These two methods are practically guaranteed to get the job done. But you should also experiment and become your own sexual Ladies' Man.

8

Your Girl Pleasuring You

"Mom, everybody loves your tetas."
—MY BROTHER MAX, AT THREE YEARS OLD

Your primary concern as a "recipient" when hooking up with a girl is that she's comfortable with what she's doing. Your secondary concern is that she's doing it the way you like it. Just like you want a girl to tell *you* what she wants sexually, you have to tell *her* what *you* want. Communicate. Talk to her. It's a waste of her time to be doing something that's not making you feel good, and it's a waste of your time to be unsatisfied.

Remember to be respectful of the way you phrase your requests. Otherwise you may be pressuring a girl into doing something she's not comfortable with.

For instance, you can never *tell* a girl to give you a blow job, but if she starts to give you a blow job, you can tell her how you like it. *¿Entiendes?*

Committing *to* the sexual act is up to her, but once she's committed, you need to communicate your sexual preferences.

Hand Jobs

Hand jobs are suspect.

Why?

Many girls don't know what they're doing when they give a guy a hand job. Guys, on the other hand? We're samurais of the masturbatory arts.

Girls can chafe the crap out of Mushroom Tip Rich by rubbing him too hard with the wrong grip and no lubrication.

My friend once told me about this girl who tried to give him a hand job when they were hooking up. I guess she thought that tugging on his penis like she was milking a cow would give him an orgasm.

One problem: It's a dick, not an udder.

She was tugging away, completely dry, waiting for him to blow his load.

Didn't happen.

Wasn't gonna happen.

Some guys like hand jobs (after all, everybody gets turned on in different ways by different things). However, some guys just let bad hand jobs continue because *a hand on the dick is better than a hand not on the dick.*

So how do you avoid the bad hand job?

Well, if she starts the hand job and thinks it's acceptable to go dry, then just tell her that you like it with lotion. Or grab her hand, take the lotion from your bedside (you should always keep lotion at bedside for emergency masturbation sessions), and squirt some in her hand. You'll only need to do it once, and she'll never forget that she needs to use lube again.

And if all else fails, she can use her spit as a lubricant for the hand job. (Side note: If you are with a woman who is willing to have her saliva double as lube, you should consider marrying her.)

If she doesn't use a lubricant, she's going to have to grab your dick in the *sweet spot:* the spot where she can move up and down without giving you a rash. Just as you would like a girl to direct you to her Clitoris, direct any willing parties to your sweet spot. Don't be afraid to tell her how you like it.

To be clear, there are only two choices here: Lubricate or use the sweet spot—it's your decision.

Ladies,

In the *sweet spot* we have a small amount of loose skin that will move up and down. This is the part you should locate and use when giving a hand job.

When you have ahold of a guy's sweet spot, you should be able to move your hand over the shaft of his penis while still reaching the head. (This is important, since the penis tip has the most nerve endings, and gives us the most pleasure).

Blow Jobs

Blow jobs can be a tricky subject. As Dick Dickens put it, "*It was the best of times, it was the worst of times.*"

Believe me, with a name like *Dick-ens*, I'm pretty sure he was talking about blow jobs. Dick was pimpin' just like Mark Twain, A.G.B., and O.G.

Many young women don't give blow jobs for two reasons:

1. Take a long, objective look at your penis. Is it attractive? Or does it look like a gigantic earthworm capable of gooey spewage? As my editor, Kristen Pettit, once pointed out to me over a cocktail, "The penis is not aesthetically pleasing. And it moves on its own. That's scary."

2. They don't know how to give blow jobs. They're scared to do something wrong. To look like an idiot. To seem inexperienced. We should all know how they feel. Many of us have felt (still do feel) this same way around girls.

Ladies,

While trial and error may help you learn how to satisfy your boyfriend orally, you can never go wrong with the "hand-and-mouth" technique. While you are giving him a blow job, place one or two hands below your mouth (on the shaft of his penis) and rub his dick up and down—however, his dick must be adequately lubricated by your saliva for you to properly apply the hand-and-mouth technique. Oh, by the way, never underestimate the power of simultaneous ball fondling.

Just as we'd like women to explain how we should go down on them, we need to make women feel comfortable and secure about going down on *us*. In other words, sometimes you need to teach your girlfriend how to give you a blow job. Ask her to try different things and see what feels good. Through trial and error, you should be able to arrive at a method that makes you both happy.

Vampires Suck

There are women who think it's kosher to have their teeth scrape along the shaft and tip of your penis as they're giving you a blow job. Let me paint the picture for you:

It's the most pleasure-filled moment of your life. You're finally getting a blow job.

Everything is going well.

You feel her teeth on the shaft of your dick.

Shooting pain!

Cringing!

Hair standing on end!

You endure it because you're too embarrassed to scream and too hopeful that she's going to get it right soon. So you take it. Razor-sharp teeth gliding along your shaft, piercing every nerve in your body. Parts unaffected by the scraping are writhing in sympathy.

You're dying a slow death, but you don't know what to say to her.

How should you say it?

Do not say, "You're scraping the shit out of my dick because you don't know how to give a blow job. If you'll excuse me, I think I'm gonna vomit and then cry myself to sleep."

The truth is that there is no pretty way to tell a girl her teeth are grating your shaft. It's like breaking up. You just have to do it. After all, a red, raw, irritated dick is not what you had in mind when you saw her lips drape around your Peter.

Say it with me: "Uh . . . your teeth are scraping a little bit."

To Warn or Not to Warn?

To warn a girl when you're going to shoot your load in her mouth, or not to warn?

That is the question.

In my opinion, it's always a good move to warn a girl when you're about to come—a gentlemanly gesture, if you will. That way, you put the decision in her hands. If she wants to swallow or spit, then she'll continue blowing you. If not, she will give you a hand job until you come.

Ladies,

You should *not* feel obligated to swallow a man's semen. Remind him to warn you before he comes— you can do this by saying, "Tell me before you're going to come"—and then pull his dick out of your mouth when he tells you that he is going to come, and use your hand to finish the job. If you love swallowing, then feel free to do so (and contact me as soon as possible by direct mail), but if you don't want to swallow, then don't.

Why would you want to warn your girl? Well, how would you feel if all of a sudden you were choking on hot, slimy, salty, thick liquid that squirted out of a girl's vagina? Probably not too good.

So there are really only two options: You can warn her and leave it up to her, or you can warn her and pull out. The blow job *pullout method* is when you actively pull out of her mouth right before you're going to come. If you pull out, she'll either finish the job with her hand, or you'll finish the job with your hand. (Or, in the best of circumstances, you'll pull out right as you're about to come and there won't be a job to finish.)

The pullout method is money.

It makes the girl not mind giving you a blow job. You know what that means? That means she'll probably give you a blow job in the future, because she knows she doesn't have to swallow. And that, my friends, is the goal: **to make the experience as good as it can be for the girl so that she won't mind going down on you in the future** (and the whole respecting-her-and-making-the-experience-as-pleasurable-as-possible thing).

EOE: Equal-Opportunity Ejaculate

News flash, guys: Girls can ejaculate. How? A woman's tissue in her genital area is swollen after she has an orgasm. If a multiple orgasm occurs, there's a chance that it will be an ejaculatory orgasm. The swollen tissue provides a juice-squirting environment. Her juices could feasibly be spewing all over your face. If this were going to happen I'm sure you would want a warning to get the hell out of the way. Take that into consideration, and give girls the warning they deserve.

Guidance

Guidance is when a guy puts his hand on top of a girl's head and pushes, or "guides," her head toward his dick (in the hopes of initiating a blow job). This is such a low-class, scumbag move, that I can't even begin to tell you how degrading it is.

So here it goes:

If you have to guide a girl's head down to your dick (to try and force her into giving you a blow job), then you must be doing something seriously wrong, Dave. You should pleasure your woman so intensely that she can't wait to give you a blow job.

You don't have any say in whether or not a girl goes down on you. It's her choice and her choice only.

I realize that when a guy goes down on a girl he expects reciprocation (i.e., he expects to get head). It's a fair exchange of goods. I put my mouth on your genitals and then you put your mouth on my genitals.

Ladies,

If a guy tries to guide your head down to his penis in order to get a blow job, stop the hookup and leave immediately. He's an asshole who's going to make you feel like shit sooner or later. Leave now and salvage your self-respect.

I understand your frustration if you're suffering from a lack of reciprocity. However, it does not matter. **You cannot force a girl to give you head.** You can't guide her head; you can't push her head; you can't do anything with her head to try and get head. Guidance is for abusive losers who force girls into situations they're not comfortable with.

Guidance is not the move of a Ladies' Man. It's the move of Asshole Man (a superhero who is a giant butthole. He flies around lending his powers to those with hemorrhoids, diarrhea, constipation, and other ailments of the rectum).

Sexual Intercourse

Okay. Now we've come to what most of the world feels is the big event: sexual intercourse. Before you ask yourself if you're ready to have sex with your girlfriend, you need to consider a few important things.

Use It and Lose It; Don't Use It and Keep It

Most guys treat virginity like it's a colony of anal warts; they would do anything to rid themselves of the exotic disease known as *virginity*.

This couldn't be further from the way I view things.

I believe virginity is something sacred. It's not something you just "get out of the way." The last thing you want to do is regret losing your virginity. Make sure it's intimate, sacred, and trusting when you decide to enter your sexual adulthood.

Five Questions You Need to Answer BEFORE You Have Sex

Before you're ready to have sex, you need to think about the likelihood of getting a girl pregnant. I'm going to assume that every guy reading this book plans on wearing a condom if he has sex, because not wearing a condom is idiotic, unsafe, and un-Ladies'-Man-like. There's no other choice.

Buy a condom.
Bring a condom.
Wear a condom.

But while latex condoms are up to 98 percent effective if used correctly, they are not foolproof. (Warning: Always use latex condoms, because other types of condoms can break or slip off easily.) Therefore, you should look into different methods of birth control for your female partner, too.

Additional birth control is yet another way to protect yourself (from an unwanted pregnancy) if you're thinking about becoming sexually active. However, even with the use of a condom and birth control, there's still a chance you could impregnate your girlfriend by having sexual intercourse. You have to accept this possibility and be willing and able to deal with pregnancy if you want to do the wild-monkey dance. Let's talk about some questions you should be asking yourself:

1.) If your girlfriend gets pregnant, do you know what she'll want to do?

It's the woman's decision to have or not to have the baby. As much as you may want her to have an abortion or as much as you may want her to keep the baby, if she doesn't want to, you're shit out of luck. You don't have a say in it. It's not your body, and therefore it's not your call.

2.) If she's legally a minor (under the age of eighteen in most states), do you know what her parents will want to do if she gets pregnant?

If she's a minor, she'll need to get consent from a legal guardian to have an abortion in most states. Are her parents pro-life or are they pro-choice? They may decide they want to teach their daughter a lesson about responsibility by making her have the child. You have absolutely no say in that.

3.) How do you feel about abortion?

If you're opposed to abortion, do you want to be taking this chance by having sex? If you're pro-choice, do you think abortion should be used as a fallback plan in case you "accidentally" get your girlfriend pregnant?

You have to remember that an abortion involves lives. Your life, your partner's life, an unborn child's potential life, and the lives of your families. You have to think about the physical and emotional stress that having an abortion will place on your girlfriend. It won't be *you* carrying a fetus around and then lying on the table having the abortion (or taking the pill and aborting the pregnancy at home). Remember that.

Do some serious thinking and have some sober discussions with your partner about where you stand on this matter.

4.) How do you feel about being a father at your age?

Caring for your child is the largest responsibility in the world. There's joy involved, but there's also a loss of freedom and independence. A kid is a round-the-clock job.

Are you ready for a kid? At our ages, many guys can't even properly care for themselves, let alone another human being. A baby can't do anything for him or herself without a parent. A baby will be totally dependent on you. Are you ready for that?

5.) Are you going to have the means to take care of this child?

Will you have enough money to support your child? If not, you may have to hit the workforce. Also, you can't just automatically assume that your girlfriend will give up her dreams to take care of a baby. Women have aspirations just like you. How do you feel about being a househusband? Staying home every day and working your balls off to take care of your child? If neither of you wants to stay home, are you going to have the money to afford a full-time nanny or a child care center?

Think about these things before you decide to have sex. Oh, and a few more things to consider before we get to it . . .

Famous Last Words

"I'm going to use the pullout method."

The *pullout method* is perhaps the most idiotic way of deluding yourself into believing that you're having safe sex. The pullout method is when you don't wear a condom and then you pull your dick out right before you come. Guys do this because they think if they don't come inside the girl, then they can't get her pregnant or contract an STD.

Using the pullout method is like saying you're going to pull the dirty syringe out of your arm before *all* of the heroin has entered your bloodstream. As if there's no way the dirty syringe can affect you if you take it out early.

This method doesn't work for two reasons. First, we all have pre-ejaculation: This small but potent amount of semen comes out of our penis early to make the vaginal area receptive to the load of semen on its way. Pre-ejaculate is the most potent semen our bodies release. So if you think there's no way of getting a girl pregnant if you pull out, you're wrong.

Second, the friction between your penis and a girl's vagina caused by penetration makes you susceptible to contracting or passing an STD. It isn't just coming inside a girl that exposes you or her to disease, it's the act of sex itself.

Let me make this as clear as possible. The pullout method is unprotected sex. Don't let anyone convince you to do it, and don't try to convince anyone else to do it.

If you don't have a condom, go get one (or just wait).

"She's totally clean, dude!"

How do you know if she's totally clean? Do you have a hidden camera in her vagina that you monitor on a twenty-four-hour basis? You don't know her history. (And if you have developed hidden vaginal camera technology, please contact me as soon as possible.)

How do you even know if *you're* 'totally clean'? Unless you are both tested for STDs and receive a clean bill of health from a doctor, it's anyone's call.

"We're both virgins."

Really? Well, what if she *lied* to you? What if she isn't a virgin? What if she was molested or raped by someone who had a disease? There are no certainties. With all of the pressure put on girls to say they're virgins, you'll never know for sure. So don't just rely on someone's insistence that she's never been with anyone before you.

"We've both been tested, and we've been going out for a year."

What if she's cheating on you with somebody who's infected? You don't know, do you? I have a friend who was in a serious relationship for over a year with a girl he thought was *the one.* He didn't think there was any way she would cheat on him.

He was a little off.

Not only was she cheating on him, she was having unprotected sex *with more than one guy.*

Life's unpredictable.

And so are the previous whereabouts of a woman's vagina.

For most men and women, losing their virginity and

becoming sexually active are very important steps in their lives that signal a passage into adulthood.

Deciding to enter into the world of sex means that you're ready for the responsibilities that come along with it: That means being responsible for yourself, your partner, and the world around you.

And remember that even if you take all possible pre-cautions, having sex of any kind (protected or unpro-tected) puts you at risk of getting someone pregnant and contracting an STD.

Having sex doesn't make you a man.

Acting like a man makes you a man.

And a man's job is to protect himself and those around him.

So do just that.

Your First Time

Everyone's first sexual encounter is weird (especially a person's first time having intercourse). This lends itself to the importance of being with somebody you love and trust for your first time. If you feel safe and comfortable with your girlfriend, your first time will be much more enjoyable.

There are some physical details you have to think about if it's the girl's first time. Many virgins are too "tight" to have sex. (In other words, your penis may be too big for a virgin's vagina.)

TALK TO HER ABOUT THIS. Together, you might want to try and make the experience less painful for her by fingering her before you're going to have sex. When I say, "before you're going to have sex," I mean like two to three weeks before.

When I say "fingering," I mean inserting your fingers into her vagina (to expand the area). You should finger her first with one finger, then the next time you're together, graduate to two, and the next time you're together, end up at three fingers.

The idea is to help her become accustomed to tolerating something larger than a tampon.

Once you've done this, you will be able to proceed.

Faster Than a Speeding Bullet

First things first: Take anything you've ever heard about sexual intercourse from the media and your friends and forget you ever heard it. The typical image you're fed of the guy on top, pumping away with the girl on bottom, isn't sex. That's fucking like rabbits.

You know why they say, "fucking like rabbits?" Because that's how rabbits fuck.

Not people.

Or else people would say, "Oh man, they're really fucking like people!"

So we've established that you're not a rabbit and that it's not a good idea to model your sex life after a rabbit's.

I shatter another myth: **The goal of sexual intercourse isn't to pump as fast as you can.** Girls hate that. You know Superman? He was probably a pretty bad lay. Why? It's not a good idea to be "faster than a speeding bullet" during penetration (for more than one reason).

And Now, a Word from Our Sponsor . . .

Penetration . . . I think it's funny (even though there's nothing humorous about it) that "sexual intercourse" is interchangeable with the word *penetration*. Why does nobody refer to sexual intercourse as a woman "swallowing" a man? Or a woman "engulfing" a man? Can you imagine how male conversations would sound?

Instead of:

"I flipped her over and I was fucking the shit out of her doggy-style . . . and she was going off, dude."

You'd hear:

"Oh man, so we were gettin' it on serious-lee and she just engulfed me, dude! I'm talking total immersion. . . . I had no control. . . . It was great!"

"Yeah, I know what you mean, bro. Just last week I hooked up with this girl and she totally encompassed me, man. I felt so devoured and powerless. . . . It was sweet!"

Now, Back to Your Regularly Scheduled Programming

You are not a drill press.

Guys are fed this constant bullshit about how it's manly to "fuck the shit out of somebody." Let's deconstruct that statement.

"Fuck the shit out of somebody."

Well, if we take it literally, it's not very appealing, is it? Why would you want to fuck a woman so hard that she took a shit? (Unless you have psychotic sexual fantasies.)

The disgusting, male, macho myth that sex is pumping your penis in and out of a woman's vagina really fast *just isn't true*. The quicker you forget about this misconception and eliminate it from your sexual life, the quicker you get on the path to being a Ladies' Man.

In closing, when the first session of lovemaking is going to go down, make it special for her. Make it special for *you*. Don't have sex with her. Have a romantic evening and make love to her.

When you get to the lovemaking, take it very slow. Make sure she's comfortable every step of the way. She may want to stop if it's hurting too much. It's your duty as her partner to be attentive to her needs. You may need to go *really slowly*. Listen to her. Is it hurting her? Ask her if she feels all right. Ask her if she likes what you're doing.

Be very, very, very sensitive.

And *wear a condom!*

After a Girl's First Time

After anyone's first time, but especially after a girl's first time, a person can feel physically and emotionally traumatized. For starters, a girl's vagina may hurt and could be bleeding. This may freak her out. I'm sure you would be freaked out if blood was coming out of your penis tip after sex.

Beyond these physical issues, emotions run rampant with any decision of this magnitude. Having sex for the first time is a big step for anyone, but it's an exceptionally big step for a woman. Guys are pummeled with the

Ladies,

To all of the virgins out there—don't decide to have sex with your boyfriend for the first time just to keep him around. If a guy is pressuring you to have sex with him or giving you the impression that he's going to leave you if you don't start to "put out," then you should think about dumping his ass. If you don't want to engage in certain sexual acts, then don't. And if your boyfriend doesn't support you, then he's a worthless human being who deserves to be alone. Save yourself for someone who deserves you.

notion that losing their virginity is the best thing that could ever happen to them, while girls are encouraged to guard their virginity with their lives.

Understand that, given this fact, it can be an emotional roller coaster for a girl when she loses her virginity.

Be there for her in every way. Hold her tight with both arms. Make her feel protected. Lie with her. Pet her hair. Scratch her forearms. Caress her cheeks. Tell her how sweet she is. And *don't fucking leave her after having sex!* No woman wants to be left postsex, especially after her first time. Make her feel loved. Attend to her every need.

Be her Ladies' Man.

After a Guy's First Time

It can also be a confusing and tough time for a guy after losing his virginity. Every guy expects sex to be amazing (expectations that usually aren't fulfilled when losing the big V). You have to understand that each guy reacts differently to his first time, and no matter what your reaction, you are not alone. I've talked to all of my guy friends about their first times and they all had completely different experiences.

Some liked it.

Some didn't.

Some didn't really have an opinion either way.

Some loved it and found their calling in life.

One of my friends in particular was expecting it to be "the best experience" in the world. He was anticipating a feeling unlike any other. He thought having sex was gonna make him a "man." He was always saying, "Every other guy in school has had sex; why shouldn't I?"

What he didn't realize was that his information was a

little off. Every other guy in the school had *said* he had
had sex. That means about 1 percent of those guys had
actually had sex.

Anyway, he decided that because every other guy had
said he had had sex, and because people always talked
about sex as an out-of-this-world feeling, he was going
to sleep with his girlfriend.

After he went through with it and had sex for the first
time, he was pretty shaken up. It was as if he couldn't
believe that sex wasn't what he'd pictured it to be. As he
talked about it, he was calm, but shaken:

> "She guided me in ... and ... and ... well, my
> penis didn't get far before it started to hurt her.
> She told me to go slow, but every time I would
> move a centimeter she would start screaming in
> pain, 'Owww, owww, it hurts!' She was on the
> verge of tears, man. It hurt. It made me feel sick. I
> was hurting my girlfriend. It wasn't fun. How
> could it've been? She was in pain. We did it for a
> while longer ... and then we stopped. She just lay
> there crying. . . . I'm not sure if she was crying be-
> cause it hurt her so bad, or because she expected it
> to be better. When I asked her, she couldn't even
> explain it. I just lay next to her ... holding her. I
> don't even know if I'm still a virgin. . . . I mean,
> does that even count? I hope not, man."

I have a lot of respect for my friend because he told it
like it was. He didn't try to make sex seem like something
it wasn't. That was the most open and honest a guy had
ever been with me about sex up to that point in my life.

When It Works

When sex works, it can be a wonderful, bonding experience that brings you and your girlfriend closer. After you have each had an orgasm, lie back and relax into each other's arms.

Finishing Touches

Finishing touches are the things you do to make her dream about what a fantastic man you are. These are the things that will leave her counting the days until you meet again.

Women don't forget finishing touches.

Neither does a Ladies' Man.

Massage

After you've both been satisfied (meaning you've both had orgasms and you're lying in bed), tell her to flip over so that you can give her a massage. If you've played your cards right up to this point, she's in a total state of relaxation because you've helped her achieve an orgasm. Now you top off your showmanship with the massage of a lifetime. And don't straddle her back commando. Put some freakin' underwear on.

One note: If you hook up with a girl and she gives you a full-body massage after you've hooked up . . . marry her. You're never going to meet another woman like her in your entire life.

Spoons

After you've given the massage, lie down and cuddle with her. If she has to leave, then cuddle until she goes. If you have to leave, then cuddle until you go. And if neither of you has to leave, then just fall asleep holding her.

Forearm Scratch

I wish all women knew how soothing a good forearm scratch can be. It takes a true man (or woman) to start up a soft, calming forearm scratch after a hookup.

Head Scratch

This is really the only way I fall in love with a girl. If she lies down next to me after we've been hooking up and gives me a good head scratch, I'll fall asleep like a well-fed puppy dog.

Conclusion

Colin's *Kama Sutra*

"We want a lady in the street but a freak in the bed. . . ."
—LUDACRIS

In this chapter I will provide you with an exhaustive amount of illustrated sexual positions (with detailed descriptions on how to properly execute them) that can help maximize the pleasure for you and your partner during sex.

Since being sexually active is a reality for many guys who are in relationships, I figured that you might as well be having good, healthy, informed sex, if you're going to be having any sex at all.

This chapter is loaded with positions and styles of sex that will make you an informed and versatile lover. And better yet, if you're one of the guys out there who *isn't* sexually active, reading this chapter is a good way to inform yourself about a healthy sex life for when you're ready to take on the responsibility of sex.

But let's not lie to each other: In the greatest of all likelihoods, this chapter will just provide you with some cool positions to imagine while you masturbate.

Without further ado, let's begin the madness of Colin's *Kama Sutra*. . . .

This chapter has been omitted (due to its extremely explicit content) by the U.S. Department of Homeland Sexual Security. (In fact, right now, all readers of this book are being placed on a Pink Alert.)

I guess you're just going to have to wait for the sequel: *A New Ladies' Man: A Detailed Guide to Sex.*

Good luck!

Afterword

Deep Thoughts with Colin Mortensen-Sánchez

Before you close this book, you have to understand that being a Ladies' Man is a way of life. If you choose to be a Ladies' Man, you'll talk, act, and think differently than most of your guy friends when it comes to life, and, more specifically, when it comes to women. You'll understand how to treat women, as friends, as girlfriends, and as lovers.

You'll know how to respect women . . . period.

It's not always easy to stand up for what you believe in, especially when what you believe in is the proper care of people who are so often mistreated. Your new attitude may separate you from your friends in certain ways, but these differences are normal, because, as a Ladies' Man, you will see the world through a new lens.

You may feel a strain between you and a few of your guy friends for a little while, but your fresh lifestyle can open up new worlds for you. Maybe some of your current friends are Ladies' Men in waiting, ready to be converted by someone strong who can lead them (like you).

Being a Ladies' Man instills the confidence in you not only to love and respect women but to deal with life on your terms. It will give you the confidence to be your own man in the midst of a world that wants you to be *its* man.

But being a Ladies' Man isn't just about loving women and life—it's ultimately about loving yourself. A clear awareness of the needs and desires of women results in greater self-awareness. Once you see yourself in every person, you're able to love every person, including yourself.

I struggle to live up to the standards of being a Ladies' Man every day of my life. I don't always do it perfectly, but I always try, and therefore, I grow. I get one step closer to my goal. The journey toward being a Ladies' Man is about redefining *man* and *woman* in order to create new ways for us to love each other. I hope you make your own journey.

Ladies' Men, coming to a home near you.

The End

Mientras Hay Vida, Hay Esperanza

Towardz A New Masculinity

I want to live in a world . . .

where Men cry and don't feel ashamed.
where Tears are not trapped inside and trans-
formed into rage.
where Men see vulnerability as strength.
Strength as compassion.
Compassion as love.
And love as respect for all beings.

I want to live in a world . . .

where Being a "mama's boy" is a compliment.
where *Pussy* is a term of reverence.
where Men strive to cry like girls.
where All men are in search of a
good pussy-whipping.
where The old ball and chain is the greatest blessing in a man's
life.

I want to live in a world . . .
where A strong handshake is replaced by a tender hug.
where Men hug each other without simultaneously hitting
each other on the back.
where I can cry in my friend's lap.
where Men don't pressure each other into drinking or
having sex with women.

where A man's strength is measured by the capacity of his
heart, not by his bench press.
where Being emotionally closed isn't manly.
where Straight men can find other men attractive without
feeling weird.

I want to live in a world . . .

where Women open doors for men and men open their hearts
for women.
where Sexual pleasure is mutual.
where Neither women, nor men, are objectified for any
reason.
where The sexist, macho, pigs are the traitors to their
gender, not me.
where I can open my heart to a woman and fill the ocean with
my tears and know that I am as manly as men come.

But most of all . . .
I want to live in a world where writing
something like this makes me a "man."

Contact Colin at www.colinsworld.com

About the Author

Colin Mortensen-Sánchez gives hundreds of "incredibly well received" (his words) talks each year to a wide variety of audiences all around the world—he speaks at universities, colleges, high schools, junior highs, community centers, and basically anywhere they will let him in the door. Colin also does stand-up comedy and sketch comedy shows with his comedy troupe, Boners on Parade. To book Colin for an event, to ask him a question, or to just check out his Web site, go to www.colinsworld.com.

Colin Mortensen-Sánchez is one year older than he was last year, lives in Sri Lanka, and is currently coauthoring a nonfiction book for young women with his mother (a Ph.D. and professor of Latino and Women's Studies), the follow-up book in the *A New Ladies' Man* series, and his first work of fiction.

Acknowledgments

First and foremost, I must give thanks to my mother and father for being the best parents . . . ever. My mother's dedication as an editor, theorizer, and all-around champion of this project has been unending, unparalleled, and totally unpaid.

Having started this book at such a young age and as such an immature and underdeveloped writer, it would have been impossible to see it through without the guidance of my mother. She was willing and able to respond to my neediness even at the most inopportune times. My mother is my intended reader, and in writing this book I tried my hardest to do justice to her politics and her vision (although I have undoubtedly come up short on occasion). Mom, you are the best mother and an amazing woman; I love you.

Throughout my entire life my father's support and guidance have been unwavering and indispensable. The lessons my father has taught me have made me a successful man and an appreciative son. Dad, I have never seen such a good father; I love you.

To every person in my life who took the time to read any version of my book, I am indebted to your kindness.

To all the visitors and fans of my Web site who made this book possible by keeping it alive when nobody wanted to touch something so "racy."

To Kristen Pettit, my editor at Razorbill, for believing in the project, for working so closely with me on the manuscript (your suggestions were invaluable to the editing process), for being such a delightful person to talk to, and for bringing the project to the attention of Michelle Howry—my positive and bright editor at Perigee—who made it possible to retain the "racy" material and bring my book into the light *as is*.

To all of the worker bees at Razorbill and Perigee who have put their time and resources into this project, I appreciate you.

To my agent, Jim McCarthy, for tracking me down and contacting me by way of the World Wide Web, for believing in me, for getting this project into the capable hands of my current publisher, and for supporting me the whole way through.

Lastly, writing this book helped me to realize that I am a writer, and for that I am forever indebted to the cosmos.

I didn't sell out, I bought in.